LET'S START PRAYING AGAIN

LET'S START PRAYING AGAIN

Field Work in Meditation

BERNARD BASSET, S.J.

HERDER AND HERDER

1972
HERDER AND HERDER NEW YORK
232 Madison Avenue, New York 10016

Nihil obstat: Leo J. Steady, Censor Librorum
Imprimatur: † Robert F. Joyce
Burlington, September 27, 1971

ISBN: 07–073186–1

Library of Congress Catalog Card Number: 78-176365
© 1972 by Bernard Basset
Manufactured in the United States

Contents

1. Field Work in Meditation   11
2. The Scope of the Subject   18
3. To Work Is to Pray—Or Is It?   28
4. My Room   38
5. Disposing the Soul   53
6. The Basic Ingredients   65
7. The First Two Steps   82
8. Imaginative Contemplation   104
9. Face to Face   118
    Bibliography   147
    Index   149

To
Larry, Mary, Jack, Helen Marie, Julie,
now at the start of a journey which must lead
to emptiness or to unending hope

LET'S START PRAYING AGAIN

1.

Field Work in Meditation

I write to you from St. Mary's, Isles of Scilly, the largest of two hundred little islands, eighteen miles west of the Cornish coast. They tell me that a further hundred islands may be added when the tide is low.

To my left as I type lies the Atlantic ocean, perhaps fifty yards away. From my desk I see the Penzance ferryboat moored at the jetty and the Island of Tresco, swathed in mist, is just discernible across the bay. Five of our islands are inhabited and St. Mary's boasts a supermarket and four miles of tolerable road.

The nearest land to the West must be the coast of Massachusetts, three thousand miles away. Americans coming to Europe by sea first sight our Bishop lighthouse and, in earlier centuries, many poor voyagers saw nothing more. In our ancient churchyard are the graves of American travellers, buried on Scilly after the *S.S Schiller* and other vessels piled up on our granite rocks. Not all was disaster for Americans on Scilly; the first Maryland colonists, on November 24, 1633, found shelter here from a fierce, Atlantic storm.

Were you to ask me what I am doing on St. Mary's, I would have to answer that I am continuing my search for God. True, I am also the pastor here, no exacting assignment, with only some twenty parishioners, seven of whom, on the off-islands, may reach me only in fair weather and by boat. Life on St. Mary's resembles service on an aircraft carrier; our complement of two thousand rarely escape from one another and meet daily in our twenty shops.

My daily shopping tour follows a rigid course. I go to the newsagent always, the Post Office often, the bank rarely and end in the supermarket, universally known as The Co-op. Should the town crier with his bell happen to be passing, I pause to drink in his red hot news. If I leave my chapel at 10:30 each morning, I am back by 11 to live all alone for twenty-three and a half hours per day. It is now two years since I came to the Isles of Scilly at my own request. How long I will remain is an open question which my religious superiors must decide. Were Providence to permit me to be buried on Scilly, I would have fifty-four species of sea gull wheeling above me and my toes pointing towards New York.

The title "Field Work in Meditation" is given to this chapter as an apt description of my aim. It also suits our local situation for, in summer, these islands fill up with students of every size and shape. They come to do field work and to see for themselves. We welcome archeologists, botanists, ornithologists, beachcombers and even divers who search our sea bed for buried treasure in forgotten wrecks. Just two weeks ago, one such wreck was uncovered, sunk in 1785.

Every summer morning our field workers, complete with pasties and flasks, weighed down with nets, field glasses, cameras, notebooks, head for the jetty and the boats. A few archeologists remain on St. Mary's to dig up an ancient Roman village but others make for one of the off-islands and a Bronze Age burial vault. Botanists flock to the sub-tropical gardens on Tresco; bird watchers, with permission, land in the sanctuary on Annet. Those searching for God hardly need a thermos flask or field glasses but it would do no harm for them to see the lovely island of Samson, named after an ancient hermit who there built his cell and did his field work so many centuries ago. In rough weather a boat trip is itself field work; as the Breton fisherman put it, "Lord, be good to me, your sea is so great and my boat is so small."

Field work is directly concerned with practice, with the testing of theories for ourselves. The ornithologist may read this and that about a particular bird in his impressive manuals but he then wants to check the bird's performance for himself. By active observation he may acquire new information and, who knows, prove that the experts have been wrong. Such a balancing of theory and practice preserves our equilibrium. It lessens the damage caused by generalizations and allows, to the earnest student, an opportunity to decide a subject for himself. When I was a boy, I envied those of my friends who passed as naval cadets to Dartmouth for these, after two or three months in the classroom, would set out to sea to put their theories to the test. How different was our fate! We spent nine unbroken years on French grammar and composition and, at the end, were hard put to it to say Oui Oui! Lenin succinctly expressed a truth, as urgent in prayer as in any other subject: "Theory without practice is sterile; practice without theory is blind."

After a life-time concerned with meditation, my own and other people's, I know that this balancing of theory and practice affords us the best chance of success. Over the years my own problems have responded to the treatment as have the uncertainties of thousands whom I have met during twenty-five years of directing retreats. Such clients came from every walk of life, from every age group and from many different countries; a retreat director would move from high school kids to college types, from housewives to nursing sisters, from the Royal Air Force personnel in wartime to the peace and determination of a Trappist monastery. Leaving the Trappists aside, the imbalance between theory and practice was apparent at every level; which of the two was the more neglected is hard to decide. Perhaps it would be fair to suggest that those, better educated, who had had the chance to study the theory, regarded such knowledge as sufficient and failed to practice it.

In a chapter about field work in prayer, it may pay us to pause for a moment to consider these two deficiencies and their likely results. Take, first, those who lack any knowledge of prayer or who are frightened of theory, earnest people who have been faithful to morning prayers and evening prayers throughout their lives. Such fidelity is commendable but has it produced adequate results? In some cases it clearly has and this because the individual in question could not remain satisfied with vain repetition and absorbed the necessary theory whether knowingly or not. A great many simple people, and I would class St. Teresa of Avila among them, acquire their knowledge from another, unexpected source. In much the same way, a pianist learns about music by practicing. We dare not rely on such an advance. A great many sincere people, faithful to the habits of prayer acquired in childhood, have no such progress to show. They never read about prayer and find no occasion to discuss it so that, though in other spheres of study they become proficient, in prayer they remain surprisingly juvenile. The constant repetition of empty phrases will never lead us to God. How great is the difference between the childlike and the childish; some, after years of prayer, are in behavior not that much different from those who have never prayed at all.

I have met a great many people who admit spontaneously that their prayers are inadequate or boring but shy at the thought of studying the science of prayer. A mock humility persuades them that they are not holy enough. Or they are frightened to group themselves with the eggheads; in every sphere of learning such inverted snobbery persists. Such anti-intellectuals must convince themselves that the theory of prayer is in no way related to college education or to being clever as the astonishing story of St. Bernadette so clearly shows. Indeed, it might be argued that high intelligence, wrongly used, proves an impediment to prayer.

If we turn to those who have read about prayer and mastered all the theories, we find that lack of practice causes many a catastrophe. In Christ's day, the pharisees well illustrate this point. The chief charge against them was that they used prayer as a status symbol and liked to pray in public to gain applause. It is not uncommon to meet those who have read every new book about prayer, delight to follow every latest theory, attend endless summer schools and teach-ins but rarely if ever pray. Or, if they pray, their prayer has a snobbish aura and is too high class for the ordinary run of men. The exclusive spirit of Port Royal in the France of seventeenth century is not entirely dead today. Concern for the occult, for mysticism, for yoga may be meritorious or a subtle form of spiritual snobbery. Aldous Huxley's *Devils of Loudun* still makes profitable reading, for the spiritual high jinks in that weird seventeenth-century convent have no doubt been repeated in every age.

Lenin's precise words were "Theory without practice is sterile" and the curse of the expert who does not practice what he preaches is sterility. Here, indeed, is a warning for me. Remarkably few of those who have written about this subject, attained more than mediocrity. St. Teresa of Avila is but one among hundreds of holy people who sought in vain for a director who could advise her about her prayer. She consulted a great many experts but to no use.

I came to the Isles of Scilly chiefly for field work, to test the various theories about which I have read. My book must be an amalgam of theory and practice but with the practice of prayer my chief concern. When I came to these islands I needed to know for my own satisfaction which theories were valid, which methods suited my case. Further, if I was to be able to help other people, my experience had to be firsthand. Very few people grasp the significance and power of prayer in everyday living or the number of practical problems with which it may be concerned. The charm of C. S. Lewis stems from his spiritual approach to such day-to-day questions as sleep, sickness, travel, warmth and food. Fittingly, soon before his death, he wrote his *Letters to Malcolm,* applying the theories about prayer and meditation to the simple facts of life. It was as a kind of Malcolm that I came to the Isles of Scilly and my two little rooms.

The questions that have been put to me and which I, in turn, have put to other people prove surprisingly down to earth. Whatever the theories about breathing, ecstasy, mysticism, auto-suggestion, prayer itself must always find the level of the man who is attempting to pray. Because one method of prayer proves helpful to other people, this does not prove that it will also work wonders for me. Two close friends of mine have been greatly assisted by yoga; after field work I was compelled to admit that it was not for me. Again, many sad people ask about prayer as a cure for nervous breakdowns, as the remedy for drug addiction and alcohol. For myself, I know the answer to such questions but my personal solutions may prove inadequate to somebody else. Take such simple questions as where to pray, how long to pray, must we pray daily? Only field work, trial and error, will answer these. I am astonished at the variety of questions that people ask about prayer. Such questions illustrate the complexity of a science which enters into the field of psychology, literature, culture, language yet remains intensely personal. Only last week I had this question in a letter: "When I pray, am I praying to Christ as a man or to God the Father?" One could write a whole book in answer to that. Another asks about silence as an aid to prayer, a third is concerned about family prayers and are these as satisfactory as prayer made alone? The place of imagination in prayer exercises many people and there are those, too, who are attracted or repelled by the language of the mystics, which seems to them highly sensual.

No man is able to give a categoric yes or no to other people; with the help of field work he is able to satisfy himself. This book is based on experiments and offers personal solutions, helpful to others only if they fit. It is dedicated to Larry, Mary, Jack, Helen Marie, Douglas and Julie who came from Chicago to the Isles of Scilly in the summer of 1970. Fifty years from now when the author hopes to know all the answers, they will be facing the age-old problems that are his today. For the questions about prayer reach back to the days of Moses while the answers lead to Eternity.

2.

The Scope of the Subject

As much of this book will be devoted to practice, it may not seem inappropriate to write about the theory first. No detailed analysis of sources will be attempted in this chapter, merely an impression of their scope. Those familiar with the literature on prayer will agree that the material is overwhelming, that we have here one of the most expansive subjects known to man. Which other science spans an area whose length is measured by the whole of human history and whose breadth reaches to the four corners of the earth?

In another aspect also, the study of prayer is unique. In other fields of learning, the efforts of more primitive peoples are of purely academic interest. Few modern artists are concerned about the ancient cave drawings, nor do the antique theories about bodily humours engage the attention of our medical men. The crossbows of Agincourt are housed in museums and there they will remain. Yet human prayer and contemplation, as found in distant epochs, are both topical and influential in the world that we know today. How many of the great religious leaders flourished thousands of years ago. A modern student of prayer dare not dismiss Christ, Moses, Confucius, Plato as out of date.

To illustrate this point and to demonstrate the scope of our subject, allow me to comment briefly on two modern books. Sidney Spencer's *Mysticism in World Religion* was first published in 1963. It offers us a modern sketch of man's aspirations and of the efforts made to find God. The reader hops from West to

East, is carried back through the Muslim, Byzantine, Greek and Hebrew cultures to end with the Sanskrit scriptures, still influential, though composed four thousand years ago.

Spencer covers the length of the subject where Dr. Mary Douglas measures its breadth. Her *Natural Symbols: Explorations in Cosmology* (1970) is concerned with the rejection by the Pygmies of the taboos and magic so popular in Bantu liturgies. Dr. Douglas finds that the Pygmies staged "a Protestant-like reform of ritual and conscience" with very similar results. From these happenings in primitive Africa, she is able to make a valid transition to the present upheavals inside the Roman Catholic Church. Her third chapter on "The Bog Irish" shows our contemporary confusion as a repetition of the Bantu-Pygmy dispute. Hers is but one example of a religious reformation, following the same lines and producing similar problems among devout people, contemporary and primitive.

Our subject is, then, enormous and no one man in a life-time may hope to master it. Prayer is as expansive as philosophy or music and giant libraries have been assembled around all three. I have seventy-six books about prayer on my desk at the moment—a pitiable number; Sidney Spencer, restricting himself mainly to books in English, lists some two hundred and seventy in his bibliography. Yet he is writing only a sketch of man's spiritual endeavor and would be the first to admit that his catalogue is incomplete.

As I see it, a true authority on prayer would need an embarrassing number of talents; he would have to be a psychologist, historian, theologian, traveller, poet and saint. So earnest a mystic as Simone Weil—born six weeks before I was—had mastered Greek and Hebrew and was learning Sanskrit when she died so suddenly, aged thirty-four. Part of the lasting attraction of Pere Teilhard de Chardin stems from his vocation and profession

19

which together built up that expansive vision seen in his *Milieu Divin*. Seven years of philosophy and theology and four years as a stretcher-bearer in the trenches went to the making of his mind. Those long years as a paleontologist in China deepened his understanding and made possible a poem that he alone could have written, his *Hymn of the Universe*.

Here I have mentioned only one or two books out of thousands to give some impression of the scope of our work. Throughout man's sojourn on earth, he has been praying and attempting by one means or another to unite himself with God. The history of such an attempt is extraordinary. In one sense, the methods used in East and West, by the simple and the sophisticated, have varied greatly; in another, both goal and method, all the world over appear much the same. Ancient wisdom remains wise today. I find no outdated material on prayer and few signs of any evolution which would permit us to slough off the primitives. Theology and philosophy may vary from age to age but the act of reaching up towards God has not altered greatly; it is a simple, unifying activity, spanning the centuries but always in the present where resides the Living God.

If the scope for study about prayer is as wide as creation, we are forced to cut down practice and application to our individual measurements. Field work implies such limitation with its Do-It-Yourself approach. If I attempt field work in prayer, I am restricted to my own five senses, my gifts of memory and imagination, intellectual capacity, experience, heredity, environment. We are all in some ways similar and yet how different. We may all derive some comfort by repeating daily, "There is no one quite like me in the world." From this we may deduce that our prayer cannot be Simone Weil's or Teilhard de Chardin's; it must be our own. To achieve such an individual expression, we need experiment and choice. In the course of this book, much

20

more will be said about liberty of spirit and about the value of imitation when guided by certain wise rules. Blind imitation of methods used by other people may make prayer into an artificial posture, verging on hypocrisy. Field work is therefore indispensable if we are to find the methods suited to our individual needs. It is most unlikely that any of us will discover a technique never used by any others but, as our experiments were personal, the choice will make this form of prayer our own.

Let me illustrate this urgent liberty of spirit in my own case. As I have already mentioned, two close friends recommended yoga, sent me books about it, with glowing testimonials to the benefit they had derived from it themselves. Such recommendations led me to study yoga, to practice many of the simpler exercises, to profit from Vedantic literature. The value of breathing control, of the balance between soul, mind and body I had discovered earlier from another, more amateur source. Were I twenty years younger, I would give myself wholeheartedly to this ancient discipline for contemplation which has produced such remarkable results. Yet, after field work, I know that yoga is not for me at the present juncture, that it would serve as a distraction and impede my progress towards God. In every type of field work one needs a yardstick; in prayer the only safe gauge is the Living God.

I mention this particular case as embracing the cultures of both East and West. Though our goal is common, the men of the West may find the idiom of the East too unfamiliar in the same way as a Hindu or Muslim might find it too difficult to adjust to the language and thought of St. Francis de Sales. Though I have been to India, felt its lasting attraction, read much of its literature, I still must approach God as a cockney or not at all. Simone Weil in this was different but she knew Sanskrit and was French.

21

Idiosyncrasies in prayer are to be expected and extend far beyond the barriers between East and West. Why, people with the same cultural background, from the same town and decade, may differ radically! Thus, C. S. Lewis expresses surprise at Rose Macauley's prayer life; he admits that her efforts are not for him. "Like you," he writes to Malcolm, "I was staggered by this continual search for more and more prayers. If she were merely collecting them as *objets d'art,* I could understand it; she was a born collector. But I get the impression that she collected them in order to use them; that her whole prayer life depended on what we may call ready-made prayers—prayers written by other people." On a point such as this, I would side wholeheartedly with C. S. Lewis while accepting that a great many other people besides Rose Macauley have been helped by ready-made prayers. Among the most popular books of this decade has been the collection of ready-made prayers composed by Michel Quoist.

The one essential in field work—I stress this repeatedly—is that we test the various methods for ourselves. If some of our conclusions prove erratic and need correction later, at least they will be our own. In prayer, we react differently. It is encouraging to note that St. Ignatius of Loyola, one of the very few saints who specialized in field work, underlined our diversity in his little book. *The Spiritual Exercises* was a book to be used in prayer, not to be read. Its hundred small pages were designed to stimulate experiment in a retreat of thirty days. Ignatius writes at the very start "that some are slower than others at finding what they want . . . some more diligent, some more agitated," and he asks the director to adapt the program to the individual need. Could much of our immaturity in prayer be due to the neglect of this all important rule? In our youth, we were preached at, catechized, instructed, examined but rarely encouraged to experiment for ourselves.

Given the mass of material about prayer and the chance to initiate our own investigations, all that is now needed is a clear understanding of our aims. How test the value of a method unless we are able to use it as a means to an end? What are we trying to achieve when we pray? Well, the shortest definition is the clearest: "Prayer is the raising up of the mind and heart to God." Here is a short and apt description of any form of valid prayer. It stresses the double effort needed on our part to lift up both mind and heart. We pray with these two vital faculties, the ability to think and the capacity to love. Many tomes have been written about this double activity, all important and a theme recurring throughout this book. At the moment we may pass them by to attend to the third term in our definition, for prayer is the raising up of the mind and heart to God. With the mention of God we come face to face with the most enthralling mystery in the world. Field work in meditation is no more than an attempted answer to the question "How can I reach God?"

The purpose behind all prayer and the gauge by which we may test individual methods is this basic human desire to contact God. In the history of all religions there is this constant sense of striving, all too often frustrated by the immensity and elusiveness of God. As with a range of mountains, clear, majestic, two-dimensional in the distance, God, as one draws nearer to him, recedes and expands. What had seemed to be the highest peak on the far horizon proves on arrival to be no more than a foothill to a range. For me, a recent trivial experience helped to drive home the point. Hiking with a friend on the coast of Cornwall, we suddenly defied each other to view the sea from the cliff edge. The height was considerable and the very thought of a fall, awe-inspiring; for the last few yards we crawled on our stomachs to avoid dizziness. My knuckles were white as I gripped the turf and eased my neck forward to find myself eye-ball to eye-ball with a complacent cow in the field beyond.

In the story of most religions, one meets a sense of inadequacy and of disappointment among those believers who have glimpsed the further truth. The majority is more easily contented, more earthy and more lazy, aware of further mysteries but satisfied to be near enough. Only the few go on. In the classical Roman world, the man-made Gods and Goddesses seemed to satisfy the people with their feasts, their legends and their liturgies. Such profound thinkers as Cicero, Virgil, Marcus Aurelius felt it to be their duty to conform to tradition and to participate in such empty but hallowed practices. Virgil saw much further and was honored by the early Christians both as saint and mystic for reaching beyond Olympus to the Divine reality. Marcus Aurelius as Emperor was deeply involved in the State religion but in private entertained a real distinction between the Gods of Rome and the Universal God.

A similar urge to press on to the range beyond the foothills may be seen in almost every religious group. Thus in Buddhism we find the division between the *Hinayana* and the *Mahayana,* translated by Aelred Graham as the lesser vehicle and the great. The *Mahayana* was considered great because it probed more deeply, and touched a more perfect form of contemplation "because of the greatness of the goal it advocated, which was no other than Buddhahood itself." In the Hindu world we find the same. Along with the Romans and Greeks, the Indians had innumerable Gods and Goddesses in their heaven but in the *Mundaka Upanishad,* one comes of a sudden on this expression: "Brahma was, before the Gods were."

The ancient Hebrews should have been protected from this two-storey structure with the lesser Gods in the foreground and the one true God on the upper floor. In so many ways they managed to escape from any such division but the urge was always towards idolatry. Where the more thoughtful Romans and Greeks searched earnestly for a Supreme Being far above Mount Olympus, the less thoughtful Hebrews envied the Gentiles with their many Gods. Idolatry had its pull for them as did the worship of intermediary angels while their liturgy became so cluttered up with rubrics that the observance of the Law almost took the place of God.

Unwittingly and with no obvious ill-intention, we Christians may also have lost our vision and the wider view. Means so easily turn into ends and because they are good, they may provide an immediate satisfaction which is strong enough to persuade us to call off the search for God too soon. In my youth, the cult of the Virgin Mary, in itself worthy and satisfying, may have obscured the search for God. Newman, in his *Apologia,* describing his hesitations about Catholicism, mentions this point. In our own day, many of the criticisms of a structured Church do no more than repeat the complaint heard in East and West throughout the ages, voiced by those who, "in a mirror darkly," have enjoyed the vision of God. One cannot read the great Christian masters of prayer without an awareness that they saw more than is now offered in an organized and structured Church.

Personally, I see no justification for such criticism of structured religion, for structures are essential in a society. The weakness is in ourselves. As we are speaking of vision, let us draw a simple example from our visits to the oculist. This good man puts lens after lens before each eye, twisting them gently this way or that way but leaving to the patient the final choice. Almost all of these permutations permit one to read the more obvious letters but one arrangement goes very much further, enlarging the smaller print in the line below. In much the same way, the structured Church may assist and strengthen our spiritual vision not only by offering a choice of glasses but also by encouraging us to make the effort to see more. In the history of human religion, such encouragement has all too often been lacking, the official leaders remaining content to let us all see the obvious. Those who want to read between the lines, to tackle the smaller print, to see beyond the façade of life to the Supreme Being behind it, must find and cherish such a determination for themselves.

Field work in prayer and contemplation is, then, a personal determination which leads us to look at life through lens after lens. The object of our exercises is a simpler but more penetrating point of view. The great Hindu writer Radhakrishnan made the point excellently when describing St. Augustine's vision at Ostia. "Augustine," he notes, "wrote a work of fifteen books on the Trinity, yet when he stood with his mother at the window of the house at Ostia and sought to express the profound sense he felt at being in the grasp of God, he spoke not of the Trinity but of the one God in whose presence the soul is lifted above itself and above all words and signs."

The above in mind, I like to begin my field work in prayer at ancient Athens with St. Paul "exasperated to see how the city was full of idols." When his great opportunity came and the Athenians brought him before the Court of Areopagus, Paul decided to begin his address on this very point. His words pick out the path for us. He opened: "Men of Athens, I see that in everything that concerns religion, you are uncommonly scrupulous. For as I was going round looking at the objects of your worship, I noticed among other things an altar bearing the inscription 'To the Unknown God.' What you worship but do not know—this is what I now proclaim."

This brilliant and baffling scene whose depths will never be exhausted, compels us to face the ultimate, Eternal fact. God is evasive and unless we set out with ruthless determination to find him, he will remain The Unknown God today. Yes, with the men of the past, we will have our mediators, liturgies, festivals, altars, shrines, Vestal Virgins without any adequate answer to the Eternal question mark. Yet I am confident that there is an answer for those who take the trouble to search. When Paul finished speaking at Athens, some of the audience scoffed. Others said, "We will hear you on this subject some other time." Paul left the assembly and some men joined him, "including Dionysius, a member of the Court of Areopagus." This Dionysius or Denis may serve as our guide or mentor; we meet him in a later chapter and he is in a sense the hero of my book.

Teilhard de Chardin may terminate this chapter on field work and its scope. This great Frenchman, who so loved St. Paul, chose the scene in Athens as the beginning for his *Milieu Divin*. "I shall turn back, with those who care to follow me to the Agora. There, in each other's company, we shall listen to St. Paul telling the Areopagites of 'God who made man that he might seek Him, God whom we try to apprehend by the groping of our lives.'"

When I came to St. Mary's, Isles of Scilly, my first attempt at field work took me no further than my bedroom wall. Friends from Chicago had brought me a simple, artistic plaster bracket for which I made a small granite altar with a miniature bundle of faggots on top. Had I been skilled at lettering, I would have added the inscription *"Deo Ignoto"*—"To the Unknown God."

Do you remember, Larry? You saw my unusual shrine and quizzed me about it; you said, "Who is this Unknown God?"

3.

To Work Is to Pray—Or Is It?

BEFORE considering prayer in its more positive aspects, let me raise certain issues which we all must face. These may be expressed in the form of questions. Where should I pray? When should I pray? Must I pray daily? Because I am busy, may I substitute other good works for prayer? Behind such queries lies the wider issue: Is prayer a spontaneous act made on the spur of the moment, or should it be a formal, measured exercise?

Less than fifty years ago, prayer was still a solemn occasion governed by etiquette and prescribed by rule. We knelt by our beds for prayer, morning and evening; not to kneel would have been thought disrespectful and a sign that we were growing slack. At school, we joined our hands and dropped our eyes demurely when at the morning assembly two minutes were assigned to God. In my university days, grace before meals was still part of the college discipline at Oxford; we lowered our heads and kept silence as on Armistice day. Should a distinguished sportsman die, we honored his memory in silence, standing bareheaded and slightly embarrassed at the start of the football match. With morning prayers at home, a formula was arrived at; my earliest ended, "Take the lump out of Granny's throat."

Not fifty years ago, the highlight of our Godly week was Church on Sunday, an operation demanding our best clothes. In Church, our prayer was worded by priest and choir, our contribution as good Christian children was to behave ourselves as best we could. This weekly Mass was a peaceful, innocent expression of our submission, less to the Almighty than to our innumerable aunts.

In more recent years, the slant towards informality has been increasing and the oldtime disciplines have disappeared. I myself have heard morning and evening prayer discouraged as a middle-class form of hypocrisy. The case against them ran like this, that they pinned our religion down to certain moments where we should be living our faith every minute of the day. This current, happy-go-lucky approach is found on the parish level in the redoubling of effort towards community, commitment, Christian charity. The fashion is for group discussion, community singing, offertory processions, kissing, organized liturgically. As to words in prayer, the goal is spontaneity. We are back to the gift of tongues and the tongue is much in favor at the moment, with a slight preference for bad grammar and the use of not too many verbs. Silence is out and private prayer if not actually discouraged has quietly slipped into second place.

This more breezy attitude towards prayer, observable on the parish level, is also accepted in the Christian home. Here, an occasional holy thought or a spontaneous aspiration shows God that our hearts are in the right place. Are we fooling ourselves? C. S. Lewis described the situation well in his *Screwtape Letters* and in this he has the older Devil inviting his younger colleague to produce the very attitude which we now accept:

"The best thing, where it is possible, is to keep the patient from the serious intention of praying altogether. When the patient is an adult, recently re-converted to the Enemy's party, like your man, this is best done by encouraging him to remember, or to think he remembers, the parrot-like nature of his prayers in childhood. In reaction against this, he may be persuaded to aim at something entirely spontaneous, inward, informal and unregularized; and what this will actually mean to a beginner will be an effort to produce in himself a vague, devotional mood in which real concentration of will and intelligence have no part. One of their poets, Coleridge, has recorded that he did not pray 'with moving lips and bended knees' but merely 'composed his spirit to love' and indulged 'a sense of supplication.' That is exactly the sort of prayer we want; and since it bears a superficial resemblance to the prayer of silence as practised by those very advanced in the Enemy's service, clever and lazy patients can be taken in by it for quite a long time. At the very least, they can be persuaded that the bodily position makes no difference to their prayers; for they constantly forget what you must always remember, that they are animals and that whatever their bodies do affects their souls."

One form of this practice, common today, presumes that all time is prayer time, that one need not interrupt the gardening or housework for, as St. Teresa put it, "God walks among the pots and pans." One recent correspondent quoted the example of Brother Lawrence who declared after fifteen years in the kitchen that "the most absorbing work could not divert him from God." This holy old Carmelite added for good measure that his time of prayer was no different from any other as he prayed all the time.

Exponents of this method of prayer are pleased to quote the Latin tag. "*Laborare est orare*," to work is to pray, has a long Christian tradition behind it and, in the lives of the Trappists, helps to explain the long hours which these contemplatives spend in the fields. The integrity with which one performs each task, the skill that one brings to one's craft or profession is, in a very true sense, an act of adoration to God. Men may become holy through work. In recent years, much has been made of

Christ the Worker, and rightly so. Christ was a carpenter. Joseph, his foster father, followed the same trade, Peter made his living as a fisherman, Paul reverted to his craft as a tentmaker rather than be a financial embarrassment to his friends. *"Laborare est orare"* remains a valid proposition in our day. For those who spend a third of their lives at work, no effort is needed to underline a statement which gives to work the dignity that it deserves. Teilhard de Chardin in his *Milieu Divin* makes this important point: "God, in all that is most living and incarnate in him, is not far away from us, altogether apart from the world we see, touch, hear, smell and taste about us. Rather, he awaits us, every instant, in our action, in the work of the moment. There is a sense in which he is at the tip of my pen, my spade, my brush, my needle—of my heart and of my thought. By pressing the stroke, the line or the stitch on which I am engaged to its ultimate natural finish, I shall lay hold of that last end towards which my innermost will tends."

In one sense, then, to work is to pray. The attraction of such an attitude is heightened in these days by the constant pressure under which so many of us have to live. The mother, lacking domestic help; the commuter, travelling home exhausted; the secretary hurrying home to support her aged parents may feel good for nothing else. The merit of seeing work as a prayer lies in its nobility of purpose; those daily chores suddenly seem worth doing which previously were a bind.

Unless we are contemplative monks, we are today subjected to so many pressures that *"Laborare est orare"* seems to offer us a valid excuse. Teachers, nurses, doctors, living under constant pressure find that they lack both the time and the mood to pray to God. Even priests and bishops are so committed to God's business that they cannot easily find the time to converse with him. At the start of the Second Vatican Council, Pope

John, aged eighty, spent six hours in St. Peter's, for the opening ceremonies. I wondered at the time how a Pope, thus committed, could possibly find time for private meditation unless sitting on a throne is a kind of prayer.

The acceptance of our daily routine as a form of prayer used to seem to me as the only answer and I adopted it willingly. Not only did I advise others to take what comes, to pray as best they could in each busy occupation, but I myself accepted the theory without a qualm. Such an attitude seemed sensible for a retreat director, engaged all day in the service of God. Public Mass during a retreat might take an hour, four conferences consumed two more. The remainder of each long day had to be devoted to confessions and private interviews. Such a program, day after day, absorbed every waking hour and appeared as a valid substitute for prayer. God, after all, was "at the tip of my pen, my spade, my brush, my needle—of my heart and of my thought." I knew that I was right and gave the like advice to other busy people; today after field work, I now know that I was wrong. A better word might be "misguided;" as when I gave a passing motorist elaborate instructions for taking the road to Gloucester, only to discover after he had zoomed away that I had sent him to Worcester by mistake.

Three cogent reasons have compelled me to admit to my mistake. First, the mental attitude is wrong. A man who says to himself, "I am not bound to pray in such a situation," or "I am dispensed from prayer because of outside pressures," or "Surely I can count as prayer this or that charitable undertaking" is taking a wrong attitude to prayer. These three expressions reveal prayer as a duty or a burden from which we may escape with a good excuse. Just as a boy asks, "Would you let me off my piano practice?," so we look around for an excuse. So negative an attitude exposes an erroneous way of thinking

32

and shows that we have failed to see the significance of prayer in our lives. That we have a need for prayer and are the chief beneficiaries is a lesson not yet learnt. Take the boy and his piano practice again. A true lover of music could never ask "to be let off practice" though he might ask to rearrange his time-table and to change his time of practice to a more convenient date. Part of the explanation of our juvenile approach to prayer may be that, like the school boy, we are not at heart convinced that such practice does much good. The boy practices the piano because his parents want it; we pray as a duty to please God. The genuine pianist cannot dodge his practice because he loves music, because his heart is in his work. Prayer by definition is the raising up of the mind and heart to God.

Prayer is a duty in much the same way as breakfast is a duty; in the unlikely event of a boy asking me, "May I miss my breakfast?", I would say No. A boy needs his breakfast to maintain his strength and growth. One might permit him to arrive late or to go early, to take it with him or to run breakfast into lunch. Eat he must for his own good. The plain fact about prayer is that I am not bound to pray every day or at any precise moment but I must not cut myself off from its nourishment. The image of prayer as food for the soul is not uncommon and it is also often compared to a fountain from which the weary traveller may drink. Certainly it is a refreshment as field work abundantly shows. We need no dispensation to omit prayer at one hour or another for prayer is not regulated by the clock. We may postpone it but we will not survive without it, for it is as important as food or sleep.

A second reason for misgivings on my part about my previous practice turns on the substitution of other good works for prayer. I would have to maintain that such an approach, apparently reasonable and unavoidable, fails to satisfy the heart

33

of man. Some years ago, an advertisement appeared in the London subways: "There is no substitute for wool." So, too, there is no substitute for prayer. History underlines this point. Over the ages there has survived a sound distinction between Christian scholars, poets, artists, canonists, theologians, on the one hand; on the other, the men of prayer. A theologian like Thomas Aquinas could be a man of prayer but a man of prayer may not be a theologian, indeed the saintly Curé of Ars had considerable difficulty in passing any theological exam. Augustine, the scholar, was a man of prayer but not all men of prayer are scholars; Ignatius of Loyola, an old soldier, had turned thirty before he took his education in hand. Were I to substitute any other work for prayer, I might lead a Christian life of great usefulness and distinction but I could never be holy, never become a saint. There have been saints who could not preach, who could not teach, who could not write or nurse the sick or catechize children; there is no saint who did not pray.

We read many gloomy accounts today of the decline of religion but these should be taken with a pinch of salt. Throughout the ages, this has been a recurring theme. My own experience convinces me that the draw towards the spiritual is strong today. Behind the credibility gap, the generation gap, the Hippies, the Pentecostals, one meets a genuine search for the Unknown God. The great publishing houses have recognized a market for their magnificent spiritual paperbacks. The enormous sales of recent translations of the Bible cannot be dismissed as an accident. Bible sales alone would not convince me but these cannot be ignored. One may add to them the bewildering popularity of so many spiritual writers of every creed. Ten years ago Thomas Merton was a bestseller and all his books were concerned with prayer. C. S. Lewis was another giant, always with a spiritual theme. One need only mention Teilhard de Chardin,

Viktor Frankl, Dag Hammarskjold, Aldous Huxley, Dietrich Bonhoeffer, Radhakrishnan to uncover in our own day a rich spiritual seam.

Our concern today should be the waning influence of the Churches, due in some measure to this substitution of activities for prayer. Where the general public, Christian or agnostic, is drawn towards the spiritual as materialism fails to produce an answer, it finds small response inside the Church. Indeed the Churches are coming to assume the role of the old Roman State religion and the talking power of the Areopagus. An appreciable number of Christians today, unable to find much satisfaction in Western religion, turn to the mysticism of the East. How many have found through yoga or Buddhism, if not the full answer, a new approach to prayer unknown at home.

The distinguished Belgian Benedictine J. M. Déchanet, who has done so much to popularize yoga, expresses this mounting dissatisfaction thus: "This does not imply a general loss of esteem for private prayer so much as a 'drought of the soul,' an 'inhibited feeling,' exacerbated by a kind of 'habitual nervous agitation,' kept going by the need to move, to speak, to do something and by the sense of powerlessness to get oneself away from the world of noise."

This author, so helpful about prayer in his *Christian Yoga,* puts a sensitive and experienced finger on the sore point. Before describing the quiet of the East and its lasting attraction for spiritual people, Déchanet stresses the noise and commotion that is killing true prayer in the West. "Spun about in the whirl of business, enslaved to countless technical inventions, man is severed from God and from the world of the spirit. *Non in commotione Deus:* God does not dwell in turbulence. To find him there must be calm within, certain senses must be hushed. Tossed around as we are, if God wishes to speak to us, his

35

LET'S START PRAYING AGAIN

voice, small and still, will be lost in the hubbub of our daily lives; the rackets and noise drowning our minds will prevent his penetration into that seclusion we call 'heart'—the living witness of that life in us which is most sacred and most true; the life we call *inner* and *spiritual*."

All this needed to be said and it has been put forward courteously by a European, trained in a European abbey, devoted to our Western traditions and yet enchanted by the quiet meditation of the East. His *Christian Yoga* provides an admirable starting point for field work as those who are interested may prove for themselves. Déchanet certainly helped me to change my opinion about the substitution of activity for private prayer. Even a casual introduction to yoga will be sufficient to prove the point. When this Benedictine priest criticizes our present practice in the West, he is not merely praising the Eastern methods but advocating an attitude to prayer known to St. Benedict, St. Bernard and the other great masters of the Western world. An essential part of prayer has somehow been lost. We do not need to turn to yoga but to the oldtime Western traditions to grasp our impoverishment. How many saints could have given the answer to Déchanet's complaint: "Go into any church on a Sunday while Mass is being said. Among those that are there, fulfilling their obligations, how many are really following what is happening at the altar? How many have in fact come to pray, to recollect themselves, to draw peace of mind, content of soul and the unfolding of their true being from contact with God? And above all, how many of those who have come into Church to pray have prepared themselves for prayer by forgetting their work and worries for a moment, by breaking free from the harsh clutch of life's needs? Very few we may be sure."

To conclude. After years of substituting activities for prayer, of "getting off" prayer for more important duties, I learned through field work that I was wrong. My reasons were three and two have been mentioned here. The negative view of prayer as a duty to be done unless one is able to find an excuse to dodge it, contradicts the definition that prayer is the raising up of the mind and heart to God. Next, the ready acceptance of substitutes for prayer fails to satisfy man's basic craving and has over decades gravely impoverished the spiritual life of the West. My third and most cogent reason must be considered more fully in the next chapter, the explicit teaching of Christ on the subject of prayer.

4.

My Room

ONE of the most profound and simple of religious teachers I introduce at this point. Without prejudice to his unique role in the Christian world—not here under discussion—I wish only to emphasize Christ's clarity as a teacher and the profound insights that he affords on the subject of prayer. Historically, too, his position is unusual, living as he did midway between ourselves and antiquity, midway between East and West.

Let us consider Christ's clarity as a start. After much reading and the study of many other masters, I find that I myself have not advanced appreciably beyond Christ's instructions in the Sermon on the Mount. Christ is neat, authoritative, exact, precise. Let me illustrate this point. Where so skilled a writer as Maharishi Mahesh Yogi needs a complex sentence to convey his meaning, Christ says the same in a few words. Writing of solitude Maharishi Mahesh Yogi tells us, "Seclusion is essential because the process of transcendental meditation, which is the direct way for the mind to arrive at transcendental bliss-consciousness, is a delicate one," where Christ says, "When you pray, go to your inner room."

In the light of topics raised in our last chapter, it may prove helpful to note Christ's awareness of the problems connected with prayer. He lived under considerable pressure himself. Greatly in demand as a teacher and a healer, he had on one occasion to hide himself from those who would make him king. On the very day when he had planned to withdraw with his disciples for peace and quiet, a crowd of five thousand invaded his privacy. On another occasion we find him praying throughout the night. His physical fatigue is mentioned explicitly in the scene at the well in Samaria and implied on another journey when he fell asleep in the boat. We have very few details of his domestic life but once in response to an enquirer he remarked that foxes had their lairs but that he had nowhere to rest his head. Certainly he never enjoyed that peace and seclusion that we tend to regard as essential for a prayerful life.

This problem of prayer under pressure is of such importance that we should pause to consider it here. Only a perverted sense of self-importance will persuade us that we have to live under greater pressure than those of a previous age. People sometimes say to me, "In those days they had less to do and more time to pray." Yet Christ's day was as full as ours and far more exhausting, given over, as it was, to the sick, the poor, the sinful, to the training of the twelve apostles and to the ceaseless confrontations with his enemies. St. Paul was probably more busy than his master, more under pressure with his ceaseless journeys and total lack of privacy. In pitying ourselves, we conveniently forget the labor-saving devices that those of earlier ages did not enjoy. Many of them still had to hunt for food. Their day was restricted by the need for daylight and, without central heating, they were forced to pass the winter crowded together in one living room. We have our secretaries and dictaphones where they so laboriously penned their letters; the letters written by St. Ignatius of Loyola now take up nine thousand pages of print. Teresa of Avila's journeys round Spain in a battered wagon kept her weeks and months on the road. Thomas More, a man of great prayer, was so busy about his legal practice that, as he tells us, he could find time to write his *Utopia* only by cutting down on food and sleep. Recently I came upon a passage in the letters of De Caussade, the great eighteenth-century contemplative. This distinguished priest writes, "When I arrived at Perpignan, I found a large amount of business to attend to, none of which I understood; and many people to see and to deal with, the bishop, the steward, the King's lieutenant, the Parliament, the garrison staff. You know what horror I have always entertained for visits of any sort."

Christ, then, was busy and under pressure in the two or three years of his public life. We may also note that he was in no sense a hermit or recluse. Apart from his forty days in the desert, he moved in crowded places and it was to the ordinary men and women of the cities that he gave his instructions on prayer. He was not speaking to eccentrics or urging people to leave the cities for the woods. Indeed, as a devout Jew, he played his full part in the structured, external religion of his day. He read the scriptures aloud in the synagogue of a sabbath and journeyed to the Holy City and its Temple for the greater festivals. Certainly he was never an escapist, a loner, a mystic in any eccentric sense. Rather we must judge him as a man of action, training a band of disciples to take his place. Externals meant much for him as we see in his use of wine, water, bread and other symbols, in the chartering of a large room, well furnished, for his last paschal meal with the twelve. To appreciate Christ's teaching on prayer, we should recall St. Paul's description of him: "He was like us in all things except sin."

Christ spoke about prayer on many occasions but the essentials of his teaching were set out most fully at the beginning of his public life. We find them in the Sermon on the Mount. He thought prayer of sufficient importance to deal with it fully at the very start of his campaign. With the utmost brevity, he arranged his teaching around three central points.

Point One

"*When you pray, do not be like the hypocrites; they love to say their prayers standing up in synagogue and at the street corners for everyone to see them. I tell you this; they have their reward already. But when you pray, go into a room by yourself, shut the door and pray to your Father who is there in the secret place; and your Father who sees what is secret will reward you.*"

I take this translation from the New English Bible but other versions throw further light on the central point. Thus the Jerusalem Bible tells us to go "to our private rooms"; Knox directs us to "our inner rooms," the Revised Standard "to our rooms." The passage quoted above with its "go into a room by yourself" frees us from domestic architecture to place the emphasis on solitude. Clearly Christ is stressing solitude in prayer, not only for contemplatives but for all of us with no exceptions made.

A number of obvious deductions may be derived from this first rule. The first, which seems of importance to me, directs us not only to pray in secret but to seek such seclusion by a free choice. There is all the difference in the world between finding oneself alone and putting oneself alone and it is the second and more difficult decision that Christ wants from us. I know any number of people who drive alone, travel alone, walk alone for a variety of reasons; it is less common to meet those who will go alone to pray. Yet Christ is precise. We have to open the door of our room, go in and close it on ourselves. The presence of God in this secret place, with the door shut behind us, may prove for many a fearful exercise. I myself now agree with Simone Weil that the evil and guilt within us makes us avoid such a confrontation; Adam experienced a similar embarrassment.

Next, we may deduce from the context that Christ's first concern in prayer was the avoidance of humbug, of the hypocrisy prevalent in his day. His frequent condemnation of this in the behavior of the national leaders explains his insistence that his followers should go alone to pray. The use of an actual room is not of prime importance and Christ may have stressed this merely to make his teaching plain. Solitude inside four walls is seclusion in its deepest and most vivid sense. In imitation of this, the Carthusian monks built their cells. Sir Thomas More, Lord Chancellor of England but at heart a Carthusian, deliberately chose a room for his prayer. Yet Christ himself prayed on the hillside and in the desert and in the garden at Gethsemani. In the Acts of the Apostles we come across St. Peter at lunch time, retiring to the flat roof of the house to say his prayers. Later in this book we may examine the variety of postures and places in which the saints prayed. Here, at the outset, the emphasis is merely on seclusion, the word used by Maharishi Mahesh Yogi in a quotation already given and so apt a synopsis of Christ's teaching on the point. A great many people lack domestic privacy. They have no room to retire to and must find their seclusion outside their familiar world. What they are needing, as Christ neatly put it, is "a secret place." Hypocrites pray in public to be noticed, we must pray hidden from our fellow men.

Hypocrisy being what it is, an urgent worry for all of us, it is consoling that Christ tells us that we have a right to escape. Such an escape, on Christ's teaching, is wisdom, not cowardice. Such is the nature of man that given one other human being near him, he will be tempted to act, to pose, to sell himself. St. Teresa of Avila maintains that those much experienced in prayer may eventually enjoy seclusion even in a crowd of people but she would not suggest this for novices. In her reformed convent of St. Joseph in Avila, each sister was given her private oratory, still known as her *Solitude*.

When one is alone, one is not necessarily a better person, only more genuine. Thomas More saw seclusion as a kind of spiritual greenroom to which actors retired in their hired garments from the heat and bustle of the stage. With no audience to play to, we may more easily be ourselves. Further, when alone, we adjust our standards of value, no longer regarding our impact on others as all important and our prayer life as auxiliary. Archbishop Temple of Canterbury put this very well: "The right relation between prayer and conduct is not that conduct is supremely important and prayer may help it but that prayer is supremely important and conduct tests it."

One final deduction from Christ's first instruction must suffice. Christ told us to pray in our rooms as a defense against humbug but it would be wrong to see this injunction purely as an escape from hypocrisy. There is a positive side to his teaching, namely, the reward that derives from sincerity. Christ said, "Your Father who sees all that is done in secret will reward you," and in this lies the satisfaction of private prayer. For the millions who want to be so much better than they outwardly appear to be and whose public performance is no more than a parody of their inward desires, secret prayer is both solace and therapy. How many of us are weary of our "act." God, like the nurse in a surgical ward, stands aloof from the newest patient, still self-important in his suburban trappings, but grows in sympathy to match his mounting fears. She sees through the initial sham to his humiliation and gradual self-surrender as he lies, frightened but far more noble, between the sheets.

Liberty in prayer becomes possible when God alone is there

to judge. St. Teresa writes, "Try not to let the prayers you make to such a Lord be words of mere politeness," and adds for good measure, "avoid being bashful with God as some people are, in the belief that they are being humble." In private prayer, the reward is gauged by our sincerity. So it comes to pass that some of those whose outward behavior is far from perfect, receive the highest rewards in secret prayer. This we may see in the stories of great conversions, with St. Paul, St. Augustine and St. Ignatius Loyola as witnesses. We may see the same more subtly shown in the early life of St. Teresa of Avila herself. De Caussade explains it thus: "I remember now that St. Teresa said, speaking of herself, that this method of prayer was a subject of suspicion in her and that what made it seem a mistake and a delusion of the devil was that the most enlightened persons whom she consulted, could not reconcile in their minds such a gift of prayer with her conduct at the time; that is to say with her eagerness to go to the parlor, to know, to see, to be seen, to chatter with relations and worldly acquaintances, thus losing a great deal of time and neglecting her soul." At the start of our field work, the Infinite God is no more than a shadow—we see now in a mirror darkly, to use St. Paul's vivid phrase. At least, through Christ, we learn this about him, that he judges us in secret with a reward as his first intent. Has it taken you as long as it has taken me to grasp Christ's first lesson, that no hypocrite has ever dared to pray in his private room alone?

Point Two

"In your prayers do not go babbling on like the heathen, who imagine that the more they say, the more likely they are to be

44

*heard. Do not imitate them. Your Father knows what your
needs are before you ask him."*

In the Sermon on the Mount, Christ seems to change our
focus, adjusting the lens of the projector to concentrate our
vision at one central point. First, he restricts the pool of light
to exclude our neighbors and by insisting on seclusion makes
us confront God, face to face. Next, in this second point, he
provides a "close-up," cutting down on the imaginative distance
between this world and the next. We like to dodge any spiritual
confrontation by imagining that God is far away. Christ here
denies the possibility of any such escape. However remote the
secret place of our choosing, God is there.

The study of religious beliefs, already mentioned, may help
to explain this reference to heathens made by Christ. It would,
I think, be true to say that the more rigid and stratified a society, the more remote will be its dieties and the less easy any
communication between the two. In the world that Christ knew
and, indeed, in most organized societies, the Gods at the peak
of a hierarchy are bound to seem remote. They act on whim,
need not heed men, use these as playthings, are mainly concerned with their own liaisons and rivalries. To win attention,
men had to make a noise. To reach the greater and more powerful Gods, they had first to contend with innumerable intermediaries, priests, magicians, witches, medicine men, evil spirits,
all of whom could trade their services to one's enemies. So
many religions were based on bribery and fear. The Gods of
Greece and Rome were remote, capricious, unpredictable and
even the one true God of the Hebrews, thundering on Sinai or
spiritually present in his Temple, was hedged about by proto-
col. The urge to buy off the Gods or to gain their ear through
intermediaries has played a significant part in much of religious

45

history. Christ's warning, "Do not imitate them," was first directed to his Jewish listeners at the very start of Christianity. He saw a danger which has remained for all his warnings; the falsification of all God-man relations through this pagan attitude.

Christ is precise. We are not to go babbling on, not to use many words because of the error that lies behind them, that God is remote and distant and needs a constant reminder of our needs. Christ himself often used petitionary prayers and in no way condemned them but he added to them the salutary proviso that God as a good Father knows what we need before we put it into words. For those who identify prayer with prayer of petition, Christ's second injunction knocks the bottom out of the exercise.

This nearness of God, if we have the grace to grasp it, must alter our way of prayer and our way of life. Its discovery for me was not unlike the upset caused by another revolution when microphone and amplifiers changed the style of public speaking fundamentally. How well I remember those earlier days before our modern address systems were introduced. The audience sat stolidly at an impossible distance and the preacher had an overriding worry, the need to be heard. Voice production was an essential art and with it went the slow, dramatic gestures to convey the meaning and those long and soulful pauses so that each sentence could be put across. Even the script of a sermon had to be most carefully arranged and studied so that each sentence could be clearly enunciated and easily caught. How difficult was the period of adjustment, how hard it was to grasp that, with a microphone before you, the ear of each listener was well within whispering distance of your lips. Now there was no need to shout, to pause, to use many words, to finish a sentence; speech at any distance could be informal and intimate. Christ's words about God's nearness make all conversation with him intimate.

The use of words in private prayer, after Christ's warning about babbling, needs to be considered carefully. Field work is required on the point. To cut out all words immediately might prove harmful and artificial; those words only are condemned by Christ which stem from a false premise that the more the words, the better the prayer is heard. St. Teresa encourages vocal prayer even for contemplative sisters but chides those who do not attend to the meaning of the words. St. Francis de Sales tolerates words in prayer but stresses the importance of the pauses during which we sit back and listen to God. One of the most helpful writers on this point is C. S. Lewis, if only for this, that he admitted that prayer without words does not always work. "I still think," he writes to Malcolm, "that the prayer without words is best—if only one can really achieve this. But I now see that in trying to make this my daily bread, I was counting on a greater mental and spiritual strength than I really have. To pray without words, one needs to be at the top of one's form. Otherwise mental acts become merely imaginative or emotional acts and a fabricated emotion is a miserable affair. When the golden moments come, when God enables one really to pray without words, who, but a fool, would reject the gift? But he does not give it—anyway to me—day in, day out. My mistake was what Pascal—if I remember rightly—calls the *Error of Stoicism;* thinking that we can do always what we can do sometimes."

The subject of words in prayer may recur later; sufficient here to note how important Christ judged this topic to be. In warning us about heathen prayer, is he condemning prayer of petition on the grounds that God already knows what we need? Here again, C. S. Lewis excels with his stress on personal friendship and that sense of intimacy with God which Christ implied. In heathen prayer, such a personal note is lacking, hence the babble of many words. As creatures we must lie passive before God but, as persons, God wills us to be active; in St. Paul's words, "to make our requests known to God." God already knows our needs but he likes to be reminded by his friends. When we formulate a petition, we participate in a truly friendly gesture, telling God that our petition seems important to ourselves. For the rest, let me quote that most helpful statement of Augustine: "Our desires are as regards God what our speech and words are as regards men."

Among the authorities on prayer, the unknown author of *The Cloud of Unknowing* is the most refreshing on the topic of words in prayer. In his quaint fifteenth-century English, this anonymous author explains Christ's teaching vividly. He devotes a short chapter to the subject and calls it "Short Prayer Pierceth Heaven" to drive home his point. Writing of prayer he remarks, "If they are in words, as they seldom are, then they are very few words; the fewer the better. If it is a little word of one syllable, I think it better than if it is of two or more, in accordance with the work of the spirit." He goes on to explain the point with the example of a house on fire. The owner of such a house does not rush out and compose a long sentence, for the single word "Fire," shouted loudly, will carry further and procure more immediate help. So, too, in prayer, a very short word "pierces the ears of Almighty God more quickly than any long psalm, churned out unthinkingly." Our author suggests two very short words to be said repeatedly, "God" and "sin."

Point Three

"This is how you should pray. Our Father in heaven, Thy name be hallowed; Thy Kingdom come, Thy will be done on earth as in heaven. Give us today our daily bread. Forgive us the wrong we have done, as we have forgiven those who have wronged us. And do not bring us to the test, but save us from the evil one."

Christ's conference on prayer, insisting on very few words said in seclusion, ends with this model prayer to guide us all. Here I have given the Lord's Prayer in the *New English* version for a different translation sometimes helps to bring out a fuller meaning by freeing us from the conventional form. The majority of people prefer the familiar phrases that they have voiced since their youth. The thought behind the language is more important and for those who normally say the Our Father only in public, it may be helpful to stress the most important point. The Our Father was written to be said in secret, free of that babbling to which Christ had just referred.

Since Christ first proposed the Pater Noster as a model, millions have fashioned their private prayers to fit this mold. Not only does Christ show a perfect economy of words and an exact scale of values, but he also blends reverence and filial affection to foster a soul-warming atmosphere. Recited aloud in church, the words may be gabbled but the contents prove bewilderingly enduring for those who savor these peacefully in their private rooms. In one of his letters, De Caussade mentions a French woman of his acquaintance who would take two hours over one recital and Ignatius of Loyola has in mind a method of prayer which takes almost as long. Ignatius is worth quoting for he demonstrates a method of using the Pater Noster with which few are familiar: "The second rule is this, that if a person, considering the Lord's Prayer, finds in one or two words good matter for thought and spiritual relish and consolation, he should not be anxious to pass on, even though the hour be spent on that one word that he has found; and the time being finished, let him say the rest of the Lord's prayer in the usual way."

There are, of course, innumerable commentaries on this famous prayer, not all of them successful, for it is hard to set out in print any observations sufficiently personal. On such key words as "Father," "bread," "forgive," "temptation," our reactions will be different. Yet I have on my desk three approaches to the Lord's Prayer by three very different types of people which have helped me to recite the prayer effectively. It would be foolish to attempt an elaborate explanation of Christ's formula at this juncture and all field work in prayer must begin with the recitation of the Pater Noster in the mood and setting demanded by Christ when he worded it. These three interpretations at the end of the chapter may serve to slow us down.

Simone Weil came upon the Lord's Prayer as an inspiration at a surprisingly late moment in her prayerful life. At the time, she was working in the vineyards of a poor Portuguese village and so moved was she, that she recited it many times daily while tending the vines. Strange to relate, she always said the Pater Noster in Greek. For her, all the emphasis is on the majesty of God, his inaccessibility. "We cannot take a single step towards him; we can only turn our eyes to him." For Simone, God is in heaven, nowhere else. "If we think we have a father here below, it is not he, it is not he, it is a false God." This highly intelligent French woman, always intense, writes with a staccato style and shoots out very simple phrases, never intended for public reading and personal to herself.

The Oxford professor, C. S. Lewis, is far more benign and

50

gentle, adding his own festoons to the words of Christ. "I call them festoons," he explains, "because they don't, I trust, obliterate the plain, public sense of the petition but are merely hung on it." Thus, to "Thy kingdom come," Lewis adds two words in italics: "*here*" and "*now*." With "Thy will be done," he underlines "*done*" to remind himself that he must be the active agent, to ask God to give him "the same mind which was also in Christ."

After a French and English approach, we may end with the Spanish attitude to the Pater Noster, set out in the sixteenth century by St. Teresa of Avila. This great mystic has now been declared a Doctor of the Church. Doctors of the Church tended to favor one particular subject and it would be no exaggeration to suggest that the Pater Noster was Teresa's specialty. Her chapters in *The Way of Perfection* are now rightly famous and not only throw light on Christ's words but on St. Teresa herself. Unlike Simone Weil who delights to have God inaccessible, Teresa cannot recite the Our Father except with Christ himself. She is a witty, motherly soul, far more verbose than our two other authors, far less scholarly but with that curious depth of vision to which few others have attained.

St. Teresa writes, "The sublimity and the perfection of this evangelical prayer is something for which we should give great praise to the Lord. So well composed by the good master was it, daughters, that each of us may use it in her own way. I am astounded when I consider that, in its few words, are enshrined all contemplation and perfection, so that if we study it, no other book seems necessary. For, thus far in the Pater Noster, the Lord has taught us the whole method of prayer and of high contemplation from the very beginning of mental prayer to Quiet and Union. . . . I have wondered why His Majesty did not expound such obscure and sublime subjects in greater detail, so that we might have understood them. It has occurred to me that, as this prayer was meant to be a general one for the use of all, so that everyone could interpret it as he thought right, as for what he wanted and find comfort in so doing, He left the matter in doubt."

5.

Disposing the Soul

IF we begin with Christ's teaching on prayer we avoid many problems and complexities. The science of prayer—as it is sometimes called—reminds me of the legal system, for though it is designed to help the ordinary citizen, it requires an expert to show him how it works. Christ, on the other hand, offers us a do-it-yourself meditation which any one of us may attempt at once.

In the Sermon on the Mount, Christ was addressing ordinary, unpretentious men and women, countryfolk, tax collectors, soldiers, potential sinners or saints. He said nothing that these could not understand. His favorite remark, "Those who have ears to hear, let them hear," invites good will rather than high intelligence; thank heaven he never said, "Those with a high I.Q. may pray alone in their rooms." Without further instruction, Peter, Zebedee, Zacheus or the Centurion could have sought seclusion and there prayed secretly with very few words. A great many simple and unlettered saints, Bernadette, Brother Lawrence and Dominic Savio among them, enjoyed high favors in prayer without reading about it in heavy, professional tomes.

One point in particular interested me when I began my field work, and I needed a full year on the Isles of Scilly to settle it. It had seemed likely to me that prayer of the type suggested by Christ would demand some adjustments and a mild rearrangement of every day life. Those whose prayer is restricted to Church on Sunday might get by without much preparation but what of those who were seeking a secret rendezvous with God? Père Déchanet, in a quotation already given, touched on this very point. Let me repeat his words for they have their importance, even for those who pray only in Church. "How many of those who have come to church to pray have prepared themselves for prayer by forgetting their work and worries for a moment, by breaking free from the harsh clutch of life's needs?" To pray secretly in one's room might demand greater alertness, awareness, balance, if one were to tune in exactly to the Divine voice. Even in everyday affairs, the man who is wrapped up in himself or too preoccupied with his worries, cuts himself off from others and is oblivious to the subtler joys of life.

When dealing with preparation for prayer and the need for adjustment, a great many spiritual writers use the word "dispose." The dictionary defines it thus: "To place suitably; to bring the mind or person into a certain state." In this precise sense, Ignatius of Loyola uses it when he describes his *Spiritual Exercises* as "any method of preparing and disposing the soul." Thomas Aquinas sees our everyday life as a form of preparation. "The Active Life," he writes, "disposes us for the Contemplative Life. We ought to dispose ourselves for the act of contemplation by calling to mind the greatness and goodness of God." Writing to her confessor, St. Teresa remarks, "I call supernatural those graces which cannot be acquired by our own efforts, however great these efforts may be, but we can dispose ourselves to receive them and we ought to regard it as of the highest importance to do so."

Such emphasis on preparation for prayer makes sense to me. In any sphere of activity worth undertaking, physical and psychological preparation is normally necessary. No great golfer or tennis player approaches an important tournament without thus disposing himself. Among writers, all manner of contrivance is used. One novelist friend of mine has to sit in a bath for half an hour if he is to reach his desk at the right time and in the right mood. An historian tried to persuade me to practice putting on my study carpet; he putts for ten minutes after each paragraph. As in writing, so in prayer I have found that any exciting diversion shatters all concentration for the rest of the day.

We do not need to be golfers or writers to grasp the meaning of the word "dispose." Most of us, wittingly or unwittingly, dispose ourselves for sleep. How elaborate an operation this may become. Some must avoid coffee for three hours in advance or take a sleeping pill at a precise moment, followed by hot milk and two ginger snaps, never three. The alarm clock must be set, before, not after, dealing with teeth or dentures, fixing the windows or testing the back door. For some a whole night of sleep is ruined unless they get into bed in a special way. One friend will fall asleep easily only if he has first untucked the foot of the bed, folded the sheet to a special pattern, approached the bed from the left side and slipped in at an angle of forty-five degrees. Such maneuvers accomplished, he is disposed to sleep.

Without becoming excessively fussy or eccentric, we may need to dispose ourselves for prayer. In this, each of us may be different. For the kind of prayer outlined by Christ, preparation is, I am sure, essential, for a certain disposition is required if one is to survive peacefully in a private room. Experiment is necessary. The method that worked last year may now prove unavailing and sometimes the habits of a life-time have to be changed. A great many people have in one day, certain periods of added tension, certain moments of physical relaxation and repose. Age plays a significant part in this as does digestion, meal times, an afternoon siesta, certain television programs, the time of retiring to bed. Men of prayer need to be as sensitive as writers who know by instinct when to apply themselves. For a great many years, I found the late evening easiest for writing; now, for no explainable reason, six o'clock in the morning suits me best.

In disposing oneself for prayer, every type of exercise must be tested and the habits of a lifetime overhauled. Thus, fifty years ago, much emphasis was placed on renunciation for a man who wished to pray. Secular distractions were judged harmful, secular reading damaging. In many religious houses newspapers and periodicals were frowned on, the walls were adorned entirely with religious pictures, high walls surrounded the building to shut out the world. The more spiritual the religious book, the more it insisted on this renunciation, the closing of the "gates of the senses" to the outside world. In his *Varieties of Religious Experience,* William James pointed out the possible error in such a course. "A mind extremely sensitive to inner discords will drop one external relation after another as interfering with the absorption of consciousness in spiritual things. Amusements must go first, then conventional society, then business, then family duties until at last seclusion, with the subdivision of the day into hours for stated religious acts, is the one thing that can be borne. The lives of saints are a history of successive renunciations of complication, one form of contact with the outer life being dropped after another, to save the purity of inner tone."

This description is no parody of a certain type of religious thinking, in fashion fifty years ago. Such an ideal of total withdrawal had held sway in the West since the early Middle Ages, at least for those who would attempt the contemplative life. The effort to avoid commitment to this world with its entanglements and dangers produced in many prayerful people the near-hysteria common to most "shut-ins." Many great saints avoided this snare—Ignatius of Loyola, Thomas More and Francis de Sales among them—but they achieved this by choosing an active life.

They followed Martha rather than Mary, while fully accepting the current opinion that Mary had chosen the better part. It is interesting to note that a similar emphasis on renunciation produced a faulty image of contemplation in the Hindu world. Writes Mararishi Mahesh Yogi, "Interpretations of the *Bhagavad Gita* and other Hindu scriptures are now so full of the idea of renunciation that they are regarded with distrust by practical men in every part of the world. Many Western universities hesitate to teach Indian philosophy for this reason."

That Christ demanded certain renunciations cannot be doubted but we do not find in his teaching any suggestion of total withdrawal from the world. His insistence on solitude and seclusion covers only the times of private prayer. If one begins one's field work on prayer with this cardinal precept, a new and restricted list of renunciations begins to appear. Certain disciplines will be required to dispose oneself for this quiet form of prayer. To achieve these, a man of prayer will have to experiment to decide which activities form a distraction and which do not. The Christian method of prayer in secret sounds very simple but, little by little, it must affect our whole way of living, a fact that we must discover for ourselves. We must dispose ourselves to pray in secret, not by ruthless renunciation but through a relaxed and peaceful style of life.

My own field work on this point was greatly assisted by two Benedictine monks. Whether or not they would help you, too, is an open question, depending for its answer on the type of prayer that you are searching for. My two Benedictines have many views in common though one is Italian, one Belgian and they lived four hundred years apart. Père Déchanet is still alive, I think, and living in the Congo; Paul Giustiniani, a rich Venetian, was born in 1476. He was the exact contemporary of Michelangelo and of Sir Thomas More. Both Déchanet and Giustiniani were attracted to prayer as Christ had taught it. "It is as impossible," wrote Giustiniani "to grow spiritually without mental prayer as it is to grow physically without food." Each admits openly that the whole purpose of his life is this union with God in the secrecy of his room. With neither of them is there escapism—William James's *successive renunciations of complication*—but a positive effort to dispose the soul to achieve a goal.

Déchanet, as we have seen, sought his solution through yoga but yoga was never an end in itself. Here was a means to an end, better suited to his purpose than those which he had learned in the West. His brief outline of yoga's five positive virtues shows us clearly why this Belgian monk chose this method to dispose his soul. The Hindu tradition, not unlike that pertaining in the West, starts with an emptying out or purification but it becomes positive much more quickly and introduces physical relaxation to attain its end. Much as one admires St. John of the Cross and the other great Spanish mystics, one cannot suppress entirely the secret wish that they had taken exercise or played games. *The Ascent of Mount Carmel,* for all its holiness and poetry, is a ponderous pilgrimage. Yoga is more constructive and positive. Déchanet writes, "The negative or passive stock constitutes the first stage of purification and on it are grafted the five positive virtues or *Niyama: purity*—outward cleanliness and purity of heart; *contentedness*—non-attachment to things and events, manifesting itself in calm, joy, a special kind of happiness and the absence of reaction to what might be called the pinpricks of life; *austerity of living*—never going beyond the limits set by discretion in thought, word or deed; *self-knowledge*—the gradual understanding of one's being and of one's self; and, lastly, *becoming attached* to the Divine and yielding up one's being entirely to a personal God."

I have no doubt that all these virtues would have been approved by St. John of the Cross. In his great treatise on prayer, we could find them all mentioned but less sympathetically. Frankly, I cannot recall over the years any emphasis in the West on cleanliness, physical relaxation, contentedness, joy as the means for disposing the soul for prayer. Déchanet offers us admirable scope for field work in the peaceful preparation for prayer. His suggestions drawn from yoga propose a temporary renunciation and withdrawal to obtain true balance that we may face life and its complexities without fear.

It is now more than fifty years since William James delivered his celebrated Gifford lectures in Edinburgh. If he there criticized some of the saints for a negative, "shut-in" form of renunciation, he also gave many warnings which have not been heeded about the harm done by tension to the psychology of man. For more than fifty years, the threat to sanity has been increasing in the more prosperous and advanced of nations, a threat not found on my islands or in other rural areas where the approach to life is less hysterical and intense. I have been forced to accept the fact that life becomes more meaningful and satisfying where the pattern of life is altered to dispose a man to relax. Yoga, with its wise attention to body control, breath control and relaxation provides a valid experiment in balanced living which we would be foolish to ignore. Interest in Yoga has been increasing with commendable results. But as Déchanet insists, yoga is not and has never been merely a body culture and those who thus restrict it, rob it of its efficacy. It is a religious exercise. As two-thirds of man's psychological problems stem from a lack of purpose, from an existential deficiency in living, religious solutions, only, will provide a lasting cure. William James saw this as do so many distinguished modern psychiatrists. The remarkable success of the Alcoholics Anonymous derives indirectly from William James and his insistence that one cannot master so strong a compulsion without a spiritual quest. Déchanet, similarly, underlines the point that yoga is a cure for tension through its spiritual approach. "It is its religious and spiritual end that is too often forgotten in Europe where the tendency is to whittle down hatha yoga in such a way as to leave only its physical aspect and to see in it nothing more than a kind of sport."

In my field work in meditation, I myself have been greatly helped by yoga and warmly recommend it here. As has been explained earlier, I find myself too old and too set in my ways to adopt it completely but of its value in disposing the soul I have no doubts. Déchanet's personal gain from the practice of yoga should lead many to study his book. "One gets the feeling of a general unwinding," he writes, "of a well-being taking hold, of a euphoria that will and in fact does last. If one's nerves have been tense and overstrung, the exercise calms them and fatigue disappears in a little time." Déchanet provides endless examples of his own physical improvement, increase in balance, ability to bear with the vagaries of temperature and weather, to brush aside life's pinpricks, to live purposefully and at peace. Above all, yoga gave him the perfect setting for praying in solitude. As "a feeling of general unwinding" is vital for prayer in our current, over-anxious setting, yoga may prove for many the first step towards disposing the soul.

Paul Giustiniani, once a prosperous business man and scholar in Renaissance Venice, assumed the life of a hermit when he was thirty-four. He like Déchanet experienced a sudden improvement in health. "I myself," he tells us, "lived a secular life for thirty-four years and, from the age of twenty until the age of thirty-three, I suffered a serious illness almost every year. Even when I was well, the price of health was very high. There was almost nothing that I could eat; no salads, salted food, tart fruits, vegetables, oil . . . the slightest change in my time of meals had a distressing effect." After twelve years as a hermit high on the bleak Italian mountains, Paul writes, "to delay or advance the time of eating does not trouble me. I feel no pain in my stomach or my head. I have as much sleep as my body needs. In fact, I sometimes have the impression that these twelve or thirteen years of eremitic life have not aged me but have actually rejuvenated me."

I would not want to pretend that a hermit's life is the answer to all life's problems or that Paul Giustiniani is a saint that we might imitate. He could, I suppose, be dismissed as an eccentric though he deals with many modern problems with a wisdom and shrewdness not always evident today. He sees the link between health and prayer, solitude and prayer, prayer and study and writes very wisely about leisure and the mastery of loneliness. For a surprising number of moderns, he could serve as a valuable guide. A great many people face loneliness in the bustle of our cities, a loneliness as extreme as he chose in his distant cell. To the old, the sick, the bereaved, we may add those who earn their living in lonely occupations, night nurses, night watchmen, travellers, emigrants, clergy, office workers, who return each evening to the solitude of their bedrooms. Giustiniani changes loneliness into an opportunity for prayer.

For me, in my field work on prayer, this old hermit gave most practical guidance on the way in which one may order one's daily living to dispose oneself for prayer. He helped me with an aside, not directly concerned with his main theme, the love of God. For this holy old man waxed indignant on one subject only, the accusation that hermits lived idle and lazy lives. This charge seems to have been common in the Venice of that day. Venice, a go-go city of our modern type, much concerned with profit and trade and highly impatient of anything quiet, could see no justification for a solitary existence or for the mild eccentric living in the hills. To one such complaint Giustiniani replied, "Whoever may believe and say that solitaries are inactive and idle, I shall never cease thinking and saying that no other life is as active and busy as that of God's servants, the hermits. For a time, longer than I would have liked, I experienced worldly affairs and the worries of governing a congregation. In these matters, I always seemed impeded more by lack of application, ability and diligence than by lack of time. With the business of active life, the more I do, the less there is to do. But in matters of the solitary life, the more ability, application and diligence I muster, the more I always find to do and the less time to do it. In solitary leisure—that is, the contemplative life—the more I do, the more I see to be done. In the active life, it is generally enough to plan and arrange matters well and then delegate the work to others. But the duties of the contemplative life must all, with God's help, be arranged and performed by ourselves. The former can, for the most part, be arranged and carried on while eating or walking about. The latter are of such a nature that each requires an entirely free mind and absorbs the whole self."

This old hermit was not unduly impressed by the pretended pressures of the busy city life. He recalls how, in his business days, he was for ever killing time, filling up hours with business lunches, entertainment, concerts, music, sport. He admits that, as a hermit, he is not involved all day in "buying or selling, building, navigating, fighting law suits," but now, from his mountain resort, he views many of these as a waste of time. Two-thirds of his so-called activities boiled down to talk. His distaste for his previous way of life leads him to write at length about his life as a hermit and in this he touches on many useful means for disposing the soul.

Giustiniani, I find, is not a man whom one would want to copy but a wise old counsellor who deserves to be heeded by those who wish to pray. Two salient features of his program prove of great practical importance, freedom of spirit and the value of manual work. As a solitary, Giustiniani was exact in cleaning his cell, his chapel, his living quarters—he laid the table properly for his frugal dinner and warned other hermits of his order to be exact about such points. I, for one, had never thought of associating prayer with such domestic niceties. Those living alone and "doing" for themselves may, through this Renaissance hermit, learn to love the dull daily chores.

Next, Giustiniani balances domestic work, manual work, reading but allows himself daily variations according to his mood. He admits that he sometimes postpones a meal because he is reading or postpones prayer because he is not suitably disposed. For him, prayer is all important and must be given that time of the day or night which suits it best. He accepts the fact that two people do not pray alike and that the same man will pray in a different manner on two different days. His method of prayer was, as he says, to have no method beyond permitting the spirit of God to blow as it wills. He writes, "Just as a ship cuts its way through the waters of the ocean but leaves no trace of its wake, so the soul, propelled by the Holy Spirit across the ocean of Divine contemplation, cannot, even by looking backward, see either the route it has followed or the point that it has reached." Christ, you will remember, told us to pray in secret with very few words. Once, when Paul Giustiniani was quizzed about his methods of prayer, he gave six words as his answer: "I adore, I honor, I thank, I appeal, I await, I desire." Few prayers could improve on this.

In a later chapter when methods of prayer are considered, Déchanet and Giustiniani will appear again. They are mentioned here for, in our modern situation, they tell us much about disposing the soul. If yoga stresses the physical importance of relaxation and the need for mental relaxation, the old Venetian hermit stresses the right use of leisure and freedom in disposing the soul. Sad it is that I had to wait until I was sixty years old to cook, dust, garden and to taste the pleasure of polishing wood. Yes, I acquired three antique pieces of furniture for my little cottage on the Isles of Scilly and found with astonishment the spiritual significance of falling in love with mahogany.

6.

The Basic Ingredients

FOR more than a thousand years, prayer in the West included three ingredients, comparable in classroom language to the three R's. Where manual work, the right use of leisure, bodily relaxation dispose the soul for contemplation, reading, thinking and praying were part of prayer itself. These three basic ingredients come down to us from St. Benedict and early monastic practice and have been used by innumerable saints. Thus Paul Giustiniani has much to say about them; indeed, it would be difficult not to come across them in any medieval book. In the middle of the sixteenth century, new forms of "instant meditation" seemed for a time to dislodge the old-time method, but this change was one more of vocabulary than of a new look.

The best account of the three R's, and one of the shortest, may be found in *The Cloud of Unknowing,* chapter thirty-five. "Nevertheless there are helps which the apprentice in contemplation should employ, namely, lesson, meditation and orison or, as they are more generally called, reading, thinking and praying." These three are dealt with elsewhere by another writer much better than I could deal with them and I need not therefore tell you about them here. Except to say this: that these three are so interwoven that for beginners and proficients—but not for the perfect —thinking may not be had unless reading and hearing come first. It is the same for all; clergy read books and the man in the street reads the clergy when he hears them preach the word of God. Beginners and proficients cannot pray unless they think first . . . Thus we see that beginners and proficients cannot think unless they read or hear first and they cannot pray without prior thinking."

Reading, therefore, or listening—surely under this heading we may include radio and television—are not merely aids to prayer but the beginning of prayer itself. Not all reading or listening is good, much of it is plainly harmful, but the author of *The Cloud of Unknowing* is directing our attention to books that make us think. The purpose of reading in prayer is to start us thinking, not the mere collecting of information as an end in itself. Such insistence on reading in prayer helps to correct that inborn error which seeks to persuade us that we have the capacity to sit alone, unaided, churning out deep thoughts. As the author of *The Cloud of Unknowing* suggests, a few very holy people enjoy such an ability but ninety-five per cent of us do not. We need a trigger subject to touch us off.

Miss Marghanita Laski in her elaborate study, *Ecstasy,* postulates the existence of such trigger subjects which fire the spirit and raise it aloft. After analyzing many accounts left by ecstatics, she draws up a list of such trigger subjects with the sea and the mountains at the top. Miss Laski extends her survey to cover poets and writers as well as mystics and for all three classes mountains and water prove the most effective stimuli. This conclusion may prove of value even in religion and in planning our holidays. Prayer in a suitable setting greatly enriches a vacation and may add a new therapy to our holiday. Here however we are not concerned with ecstasy. I mention Miss Laski because in her case histories may be found many stories in which reading supplied the trigger subject for prayer. Off the cuff, one may mention St. Augustine, John Wesley and St. Ignatius of Loyola, nor should I omit the part played by the writings of Pico della Mirandola in fashioning the sanctity of Sir Thomas More. Right reading and right listening must prove for most of us imperative for effective prayer.

Obviously there will be many occasions when anyone of us will be able to pray without a book. Granted Divine inspiration, we need no trigger subject from another source. The thief on the Cross voiced one of the most profound of prayers that man has ever uttered and yet he may well have been illiterate. Lying on one's little trolley, waiting for a surgical operation, one may pray with the thief and without a book. Spontaneous prayer is easy when a critical situation serves as a trigger subject and starts us off. But Christ told us to go to our private rooms and, as often as not, a private room affords us no adequate stimulus. God may supply this but, as often as not, he does not.

As reading is normally essential to prayer, a great many saints and spiritual writers have left to us their considered advice. The subject is highly personal and we, each of us, must make our own choice. Hurried reading, informative reading, fashionable reading is here off the point. The author of *The Cloud of Unknowing* gives us a guideline, pointing out that the end of prayer is "a sudden perception and awareness" and that this "is better learned from God than men." Bright ideas in books may not make good prayers. We read to sharpen our perception and awareness, not to heighten our sense of cleverness. Our reading must be genuine. Ignatius of Loyola asks that the age, learning and talents of each retreatant be considered "lest the untutored or those of weak constitution overburden themselves." Elsewhere in his *Spiritual Exercises* he writes, "It is not to know much but to understand and savor the matter interiorly that fills and satisfies the soul." Is there need to emphasize the point further, seeing that we have already quoted St. Teresa's statement that given the Our Father, she could see no need for any other book?

On the subject of reading in prayer, we must do our field work and experiment for ourselves. I now accept wholeheartedly that reading in prayer differs from reading for study, both in quality and quantity. The majority of great writers on prayer express their worry lest anyone should turn prayer into an intellectual exercise. Too much emphasis on reading in prayer might scare away those who are not "the reading type." Not a few of the saints may be thus described. Until printing was invented, books were hard to come by and many great saints and mystics reached the highest perfection without our modern libraries. One need not be intelligent to pray but one has to be thoughtful and such thoughtfulness should guide our choice of books. Were we to pick books which increased our perception and awareness and books which were truly thoughtful, we would achieve much.

Christ warned us about hypocrisy in prayer and such a warning must surely cover our books. At all costs, we must avoid being spiritual snobs. Wrong reading may produce this odious state of which an obvious symptom is insistence only on the latest books. From the latest books we so easily pass to the current fashion and to chasing after the spiritual director who is popularly reckoned to be "the last word." The Athenians who laughed at St. Paul were of this type. "The one amusement the Athenians and the foreigners living there seem to have," writes St. Luke, "apart from discussing the latest ideas, is listening to lectures about them."

Thomas à Kempis, writing about the use of the Sacred Scriptures, touches on this very point. "It is for truth, not for literary excellence, that we go to Holy Scripture; every passage of it ought to be read in the light of that inspiration which produced it, with an eye to our soul's profit, not to cleverness of argument. A simple book of devotion ought to be as welcome to you as any profound and learned treatise; what does it matter whether the man who wrote it was a man of great literary accomplishments? Do not be put off by his want of reputation; here is truth unadorned to attract the reader. Your business is with what the man said, not with the man who said it . . . you will get most out of it if you read it with humility and faith, not concerned to make a name for yourself as a scholar."

Armed with such humility, simplicity and faith as Thomas à Kempis has recommended, we set out to pick our books for ourselves. We require books that heighten our perception and awareness, that are thoughtful and lead us to the truth. My own field work in prayer has led me to accept these three requirements but with a further condition which I would like to explain. We must, I think, accept a fact already mentioned, that before the age of printing, there were very few books. Throughout the Middle Ages, the majority of manuscripts came from the monasteries. Not all but most of these manuscripts dealt with spiritual subjects, the Scriptures, prayer, theology and philosophy. The great medieval saints and mystics, St. Bernard, St. Bonaventure, St. Anselm, read little else. In the devout Catholic world of the Reformation, the emphasis was still placed on the value of spiritual books. Poor Ignatius, a wounded soldier lying in pain, read through the Gospel because, in his castle at Loyola, he could find little else. In his case the result was astonishing but so restrictive a choice of reading matter might not be apt for us.

After the discovery of printing, books increased rapidly and extended sensationally in their scope. The old prejudice however survived that holy people should limit themselves to holy reading and that prayer demanded the exclusion of secular books. By the Victorian age, a rigid division between secular and spiritual reading had been recognized. A visit to a Victorian spiritual library is a haunting experience. There one may see thousands and thousands of books, none of them bad, many of them excellent, but all restricted to the spiritual life. From such libraries many priests, nuns and layfolk chose the bulk of their reading or that part of their reading which they regarded as holy and worthwhile. It was not that a good Christian was not allowed to read anything else but he had to find other books in secular libraries and could not persuade himself easily that such secular reading would assist him in his prayer. Further, the authors of spiritual books tended to quote chiefly from other spiritual authors and to exclude from their material topics which might be judged as secular. A great many Christian authors were men of urbanity, scholarly men of considerable learning and undoubted taste. Such an author was St. Francis de Sales but his wider talents rarely appear in his spiritual writings and he rarely comments on history, politics, secular studies, poetry, in his devout books. The letters of De Caussade are encouraging and profound but free of any trace of humor and exhausting in their ruthless, undeviating piety. Père Grou, a man of prayer and rich in spiritual insight, was also a classical scholar of distinction, but though he published secular books of recognized merit, he rarely mentions the classics in his spiritual tomes. Our dear friend, Paul Giustiniani, a Renaissance scholar, had for long been devoted to the works of Seneca. For some unexplained reason, he almost frowned on the classics once he had become a hermit and suggests the life of a saint for light reading before going to bed. One cannot condemn such an attitude, or prove it wrong or recommend the opposite to prayerful people, but I find reasons enough in my own field work for widening my choice of reading books.

In one of his letters, Sir Thomas More suggests a division of reading other than that between the spiritual and the secular. His verdict on books would turn on the assessment, books that lead me to God and books that do not. Such a theory has much to commend it and has certainly helped me very much. With prayer in our private rooms as the goal for our reading, such terms as "spiritual" and "secular" lose much of their point. I could inspect an old-time spiritual library and reject half the volumes because they do not lead me to God. Such a rejection does not imply that the discarded books are not good or useful, indeed one might well be using them for research and study, day after day. The great treatises on dogma, canon law, liturgy, apologetics may rightly be classed as Spiritual Reading without in any way helping us to pray. Why, there are books about prayer itself which prove unhelpful and will lead us to God only in a roundabout way. Père Poulain's classic serves for me as a case in point. His *The Graces of Interior Prayer* analyzes mystical prayer in all its stages but would prove of small use to me in my private room. On the other hand, Dag Hammarskjöld's *Markings,* a slight collection of random jottings, proves enough to trigger me off.

As the years pass by, I have noted a curious literary trend which seems to support my point. Among the most enduring and popular of spiritual writers in the English speaking world of letters, the majority received their early education in a wider, non-sectarian, secular world. Men of the type of Newman, Chesterton, Chapman, Merton, Knox, Waugh, Lafarge, Martindale, Benson, Gerald Manley Hopkins were reared on the Roman and Greek classics and came to the Church mature. Their approach resembles that of Aldous Huxley, C. S. Lewis, Simone Weil, Teilhard de Chardin who drew their faith and inspiration from many spheres of learning, not purely from the earnest study of officially spiritual books. In the early Christian centuries, the same situation may be observed. Augustine's conversion began with the reading of Cicero. Virgil was regarded as a saint by the early Christians, for this great poet appeared as a precursor, groping towards the truth of the Word made flesh. Ambrose, Jerome and others were reared on the pagan classics and the same was not uncommon at a much later point in history. Thus Thomas

More, a Renaissance scholar, gave many years to the study of ancient writers, Latin and Greek. There survives a letter from John Henry Newman recommending Horace and Lucretius rather than à Kempis to an inquirer searching for God. One must not over-emphasize the point but nor must one neglect it; spiritual reading is good but the wider sphere of learning may help to sharpen our perception and so lead us to pray.

In our more modern times we face a further problem which men of the type of Augustine or Aquinas never met. Where the author of *The Cloud* included listening to sermons as a substitute for reading, we today have the television screen. Surely it is right to ask how far radio and television may help or spoil our prayer? Must we assume the attitude of those earnest Christians who condemn television outright as a distraction and an impediment to prayer? David Wilkerson in his *The Cross and the Switchblade* reached his own decision on the point: "'How much time do I spend in front of the screen each night?' I wondered. 'A couple of hours at least. What would happen, Lord, if I sold that TV set and spent that time praying?' I was the only one in the family who watched TV anyway. What would happen if I spent two hours every single night in prayer? It was an exhilarating idea. Substitute prayer for television and see what happens. Right away I thought of objections to the idea. I was tired at night. I needed the relaxation and change of pace. Television was part of our culture; it was not good for a minister to be out of touch with what people were seeing and talking about." This example is a good one and the writer, after doing his field work, sold his television set. Yet, at about the time when I read Wilkerson's splendid book, I had a card from a devout teacher: "In my situation TV is not a luxury but a necessity." Liberty of spirit in reading and listening is essential in the search for God.

For reasons which I hope to explain later, I kept my TV set as a positive aid to prayer.

The answer to such a question as this and, indeed, to every query about prayer and reading must be sought in the exact definition of our goal. Unless we are sure of our purpose in prayer, how adapt means to attain our ends? Some people pray simply from a sense of duty and no reading will greatly affect them. Others pray for an emotional release, built mainly on feelings, that sense of love and security that prayer sometimes evokes. These often turn for reading to books of a subjective type which deal with fears, scruples, doubts, examination of conscience or to theories about positive thinking and success. For me such books tend to produce self-centered prayer and much self-pity and turn prayer into a boomerang. Those who have absorbed Christ's instructions about prayer in secret need special types of reading, for it takes some courage and assurance to meet God. Day after day they face the drama of a life-time, the repetition of that awesome story of Moses before the burning bush. Reading for those who pray like this is priceless; they must read or meet God with an empty mind. St. Paul gives us a clue in this regard: "Surely I should pray not only with the spirit but with the mind as well."

The medieval scholastics had a favorite saying: "You cannot love someone whom you do not know." This axiom may be verified in every human friendship; as we come to know each other better, we either part company or love each other more. Love is a capacity distinct from knowledge but linked to knowledge, needing an increase of knowledge if it is to grow. On this point, I like the description given by Professor E. Allison Peers in his lecture on *The Imitation of Christ.* "You know how, in the process of making a friend, you learn first one thing about him and then another and so, gradually, you find yourself drawing closer to him; and then, twelve months later, you look back and think, 'Fancy, a year ago, I thought I knew him quite well when really I hardly knew him at all.'" Professor Allison Peers sees *The Imitation of Christ* as giving us this kind of knowledge of Jesus; there are other books that achieve the same for the Unknown God.

At the start of our field work, we watched St. Paul in Athens, commenting on the unexpected altar to the Unknown God. Paul maintained that the Athenians could get to know this God—his whole sermon was on this subject—and yet no saint in history has described more profoundly the incomprehensibility of God. The more that I know of God, the more will I love him, and the more I love him the more will I want to know. With God there is no end to the search in this world and yet Paul gave us a limited objective: he wrote to the Corinthians: "Now we see only puzzling reflections in a mirror but then we shall see face to face. My knowledge now is partial, then it will be whole, like God's knowledge of me." The one purpose of reading in prayer is to probe, interpret, define this puzzling reflection, the faint and obscure impressions that our world reveals.

The temptation for most of us is to abandon too easily what must seem to us an exhausting and fruitless enterprise. We give up too soon or accept as sufficient the blurred impression of the Athenians. They sat back contented with their army of idols and an altar topped by a question mark. The Hebrew doctors probed further, aided by the revelations granted to Moses, but here again they stopped too soon with the Temple and the Law. The Bible itself seemed to them the end of the story where it was but the beginning for St. Paul. Paul told the Corinthians that sooner or later the spirit of God would take over and then the earnest pilgrim would leave the foothills for the peaks. Books, like binoculars, do not lessen the obstacles on our journey but they give us courage by showing us the glory of the peaks.

How read about God? In recent years as a result of field work, I have found for myself a satisfactory formula. My choice may not be yours but, as we share the common purpose, my experience may aid you in your search. I turn back on St. Paul because he, of all the great masters of prayer, seemed to enjoy a further vision, a vision which embraced the universe. Here was a remarkable man with a single purpose which led so very far afield. Thus, at Athens and elsewhere, he was able to appreciate the sincerity and earnestness of the pagan world about him and their universal desire for the truth. He was familiar with Roman and Greek culture and was probably well versed in their literature. Yet as "a pharisee of pharisees"—to use his own expression, he was steeped in the grand traditions of his own people and scrupulous in his observance of the Law. He never rejected Jewry but he outgrew it or, better, saw it leading men to greater freedom on a higher plane. This evolution led him to Christ, the inspiration of his life. Yet, in a true sense, Paul's search did not end with the man Christ. Always for him there was the further vision of reality. From Christ, Paul climbed to the power and impulse of Christ's spirit and he seems to me the Pentecostal par excellence. With the aid of this all powerful force, Paul came nearer than any other to discerning the blurred impression in the mirror, the reflection of the living God. This unique confidence in Paul is preserved in his literary style. Keeping close to him, one dodges all overtones and undertones, is freed from emotion, imagination, prejudice or wishful thinking and may glimpse the further, cold reality ahead.

Paul wrote many startling passages about this further vision and each of us may choose our own. I take the one which has intrigued me most. When, as a small boy, I was given my first autograph book as a birthday present, I invited my parents to write on the opening pages and my father picked the passage from Paul that I now quote. But my father used the old Douai version where I now prefer the translation given by Ronald Knox.

"How deep is the mine of God's wisdom, of his knowledge; how inscrutable are his judgments, how undiscoverable his ways. Who has ever understood the Lord's thoughts or been his counsellor? Whoever was the first to give and so earned his favour? All things find in him their origin, their impulse, the centre of their being; to him be glory throughout all ages, Amen."

A passage such as this to the Romans could determine our prayerful reading for a life-time, restricting us not just to officially spiritual subjects but to the history of our universe. Words such as "inscrutable" or "undiscoverable" warn us against the slick solution, remind us of the million mysteries ahead. At the end of a life-time, we may still be seeing in a mirror darkly but, as with binoculars, our reading will have made vague impressions more clear. Over the years, a right choice of books will help to uncover a subtle pattern into which we may fit our present disjointed impressions of Justice, Love, Beauty and Truth.

In a book of this type, it would be foolish indeed to attempt a program of spiritual reading based on St. Paul's inspired text. We ourselves all differ and many books pass out-of-date. That great books survive is certain but even these suffer certain periods of neglect. One had seen Newman pass out of favor only later to return. If from Paul's passage we select certain words —the mine of God's wisdom; inscrutable; undiscoverable; their origin; their impulse; the center of their being—we may begin to see how wide our reading may be. Books about the voyage to the moon, books of astronomy, psychology, botany, history, biography, poetry may all add their meaning to Paul's words. Given prayer to God for help, I see no problem in reading slowly the works of believers and unbelievers, for most of those who call themselves agnostic are asking with Pontius Pilate, "What is truth?"

You cannot love someone whom you do not know and though it is true that on earth we will never know God completely, yet reading about life in all its facets will bring us face to face with his mysteries. It was Carlyle who said, "Wonder is the basis of worship," and books that reveal this life and its wonders will certainly lead us to pray. If science seems to have explained so many of the wonders that baffled our ancestors, it has left new and more profound wonders in its trail. Christ said, "Let your eye be simple," and for those who have this singleness of vision, thousands and thousands of books deal with the mysteries worded by St. Paul.

I still meet people whose early training taught them that there was something vaguely wrong about reading during prayer. For some three hundred years the majority of prayerful Catholics were advised to use a method of meditation based almost entirely on personal thought and bright ideas. One knelt or sat very still and sought to elicit holy thoughts. Those who tried this method enjoyed a certain satisfaction at the start. Clever thoughts came at first and with them were suitable emotions but, alas, the initial impulse soon faded leaving behind an incurable void. Some spiritual directors saw in this void a time for testing and urged on their clients to continue with such monotony for years. Other directors, rather more enlightened, advised meditative reading, an exercise in which one read a short passage from the Scriptures slowly then turned it over and chewed the cud. For certain people in certain situations such meditative reading seems to work. Its weaknesses are clear, based as it is on secondhand thoughts, overemphasis on thinking, with the added temptation to mix study up with prayer. As a student "gets up" on Shakespeare so I found myself "getting up" on God. Far greater relief for me has come from the old monastic formula of *reading, thinking, praying,* taken separately if necessary, with a space to keep them apart. For some of the old monastic writers, the chanting of the psalms in choir served as spiritual reading about which they pondered in secret later in the day. The *instant* meditation of my youth now seems to me too urgent, too prepared. How different is the attitude of the history student, mugging up a period, a reign, a campaign, a battle and that of the mature historian who has absorbed his subject by wide and leisurely reading throughout his life.

If our minds are, in Thomas More's vivid phrase, "to Godwards," then almost any book will help to illuminate our central theme. One must however have a central theme. In my books I now require (a) an increase of perception and awareness; (b) treatment of trigger-subjects; (c) the search for truth rather than for novelty or information; (d) a valid contact with one word or another in that magnificent passage by St. Paul. (e) Secondhand prayers and meditations do not often help me and I prefer books which provoke my personal thought. One final requirement, one final danger has emerged from my field work and with this we may end a chapter concerning prayerful books.

If reading is to assist in prayer, even to initiate it, we must avoid fragmentation and the trivial. The trivial in reading, in conversation and in television is that which is purely time-killing and so lacks any central theme. "Yes, but this is harmless," you may say, but in so saying, you make a serious mistake. To fill one's mind with rubbish is to foster mental dissipation, to squander or fritter away that very gift which establishes the ascendency of man. Such dissipation generates a peculiar type of boredom and if maintained for long will produce a state of mental atrophy. A surprisingly large number of men and women have so damaged their mental powers that in middle age they are more juvenile than they were as kids at school. Not many are honest enough to admit this. Years ago, a competent and elderly priest expressed to me his fear and boredom at the very thought of making his annual retreat. "It isn't that I do not love God," said he, "but the plain fact is that I have not read a book for twenty years."

The ancient writers about prayer made much of discipline and austerity, urging their disciples to cut out every kind of amusement and entertainment that might distract them in their prayer. William James has already been quoted in disapproval of so rigid an attitude. In our modern times, we may feel inclined to agree with William James and to regret such inflexibility which excluded history, poetry, secular culture from spiritual reading books. The old writers may have been too ruthless in their demands for singleness of purpose but they were right in linking mental discipline with private prayer. Restlessness in prayer, distractions, the inability to relax for half an hour derives less from ill-intention, more from habitual triviality. There is scope for much field work on this point. For myself, I was very much helped by a remark from Simone Weil on this very subject in a paper that she wrote about work at school. "The key to the Christian concept of studies is the realization that prayer consists of attention. It is the orientation of all the attention of which the soul is capable towards God. The quality of the attention counts for much in the quality of the prayer. Warmth of heart cannot make up for it."

As a man on a diet experiments with his food, substituting

one low-calorie dish for another without increasing his carbo-
hydrates, so we may ring the changes with our books, television
programs, correspondence, conversation with an increase of attention as our object and mental dissipation as the evil to be
avoided at any cost. If in prayer by myself I am to pay attention
to God, I must practice mental discipline. In my own case, I
have found that a television program of an evening proves a
very effective form of relaxation and as such, a positive aid in
prayer. Personally, I exclude no program, documentary, educational, comic, dramatic or bloody which stimulates my full attention and offers me a theme. Those programs are pernicious
on television or on radio which have no theme, reach no cathar-
sis and merely fragment the mind. Bursts of noise, snatches of
music, weather reports, commercials, news headlines, gossip all
mixed up together, cultivate inattention and make prayer impossible. Newspapers and glossies with their cartoons, advertise-
ments and gossip may prove more damaging than TV. When
I first came to the Isles of Scilly, I found with dismay that
there would be no Sunday papers and for some months I puzzled how I would fill up that day. Holiday makers from all
round the world wander about stunned and discontented of a
Sunday, missing their weekly dish of tripe. Very soon I discovered that I not only knew as much without the Sunday paper
but that my mind was very much more attentive, free of such
trivialities. Now I would not read a Sunday paper if I could.
In fact, the Sunday papers reach the Isles of Scilly on Monday
or Tuesday and what had once seemed red-hot news on Sunday
now, twenty-four hours later, looked uninvitingly stale.

If we wish to pray well, then reading is vital, any reading
that helps us to pay attention and to maintain our search for
God. The wider the scope of our reading, the more likely we
are, when *gazing in the mirror darkly,* to discern the impression

80

of the living God. Let Simone Weil say the last words about spiritual reading for hers was extensive, attentive, purposeful and precise. "For it seemed to me certain, and I still think so today, that one can never wrestle enough with God if one does so out of pure regard for truth. Christ likes us to prefer truth to him because, before being Christ, he is truth. If one turns aside from him to go towards the truth, one will not go far before falling into his arms . . .

"After this I came to feel that Plato was a mystic and all the *Iliad* is bathed in Christian light and that Dionysius and Osiris are in a certain sense Christ himself; and my love was thereby doubled. In the spring of 1940, I read the *Bhagavat Gita*. Strange to say it was in reading those marvellous words, words with such a Christian sound, put into the mouth of an incarnation of God, that I came to feel strongly that we owe an allegiance to religious truth which is quite different from the admiration we accord to a beautiful poem; it is something far more categorical . . . You can take my word for it, too, that Greece, Egypt, ancient India and ancient China, the beauty of the world, the pure and authentic reflections of this beauty in art and science, what I have seen of the inner recesses of human hearts where religious belief is unknown, all these things have done as much as the visible Christian ones to deliver me into Christ's hands as his captive" (Letter to Père Perrin).

7.

The First Two Steps

WITH all the preliminaries completed, we may now enter our private rooms. We should pause at the door. Ignatius of Loyola, ever practical, suggests that we put to ourselves this question: "Where am I going and what for?" For many years I neglected this formula as unnecessary but never now. If, as Simone Weil maintains, prayer is largely concerned with attention, then it becomes important to pay attention at the start. In reply to the question "Where am I going and what for?" I think first of the instruction given by Paul to Timothy: "This first of all I ask, that petition, prayer, entreaty and thanksgiving should be offered for all mankind."

When we pray in secret with none but God present, we are free to discard all pretensions and to pray simply as men. In seclusion, the barriers seem less important between priest and layman, man and woman, Catholic and Protestant, Muslim and Hindu. We all are creatures in our search for God and truth. Such fellowship in hope provides for me a mounting attraction as I enter my inner room. To the question "Where are you going and what for?" I reply with St. Paul about entreaty and thanksgiving for all mankind but like to add a rider: "I am going to meet God as my Father Adam used to do." With such a thought, my solitary prayer ceases to seem isolated but becomes part of the history of the world.

To emphasize our brotherhood in prayer—a fact of sweet and urgent importance, I would like to quote a passage which moved me greatly and which might have been written by Augustine, Bernard, or Thomas More. Radhakrishnan says, "In practical religion, Hinduism recognizes that there are those who wish to see God face to face, others who delight in the endeavor to know the truth of it all. Some find peace in action, others in non-action. A comprehensive religion guides each along his path to the common goal, as all woo the same Goddess though with different gifts. We must not give supreme and sole importance to our specialty. Perfection can be attained as a celibate or a householder or an anchorite. A rigid, uniform outlook is wrong. The saintliness of the holy man does not render the steadfastness of the devoted wife or the simple innocence of the child superfluous. The perfection of every type is Divine. "Whatsoever is glorious, good, beautiful and mighty, understand that it goes forth from out of the fragment of my splendor."

Liberty of Spirit

Radhakrishnan's quotation is from the *Bhagavad Gita*. The great Hindu writer here stresses a point that has been so often mentioned in these pages, the need for absolute liberty of spirit in private prayer. There truly are no rules save Christ's two suggestions, secrecy and very few words. These two, far from restricting our prayer, free us from convention, from Scripture readings or liturgical formulae. When praying alone we are entirely free to pray as the spirit moves us inside the framework of reverence. When dealing with the Our Father alone, reverence is essential but this itself may differ greatly from the reverence and decorum proper to church.

Once I have shut my door and am praying in private, no one has the authority to tell me what I must do. No Pope or bishop, parent or guru, confessor or superior, liturgist or spiritual writer is able to instruct me on how to approach my God. With public prayer, the situation is different. The liturgy is a public, social act of great value, proper to a community and governed by a common law. In an assembly, the Church may tell me where to stand, what words to say, what gestures to make, what clothes to wear, what gifts to offer; and my willingness to sink my independence and to unite with other human beings makes our act of worship significant. The current attacks on institutional and structured religion seem to me juvenile. In the books of Numbers and Deuteronomy, God prescribed detailed rubrics for the Hebrew act of worship and St. Paul was strict about this in the early Christian Church. Small honor is paid to God by those who set out to be eccentric when joining with others for public worship in a community.

In our private rooms, however, the situation is reversed. Now we must judge for ourselves and be ourselves. Our Father who sees what is done in secret alone knows the motives behind what we say and do. Absolute freedom in private prayer is essential, a point that so many of the saints have stressed. In her *Book of Foundations,* St. Teresa rebukes those who restrict their own liberty through scruples or a false conscience and compares them to the wheel of her waggon caught "in a marsh or bog from which we cannot escape." The author of *The Cloud of Unknowing* is still more vehement. Writing of contemplation, he stresses this liberty of spirit in a startling passage that throws all discretion to the winds: "If you ask me what discretion you should exercise in this work [contemplation], my answer is, "None whatever!" In everything else you do, you have to use your own discretion as, for example, in the matter of food and drink and sleep and keeping warm or cool, the time you spend in praying and reading, your conversations with your fellow Christians. In all these you have to use discretion so that they

84

are not too much or too little. But in this work cast discretion to the wind."

What We Learn From the Saints

When praying alone to God in our rooms, we have Christ's words to guide us but are under no obligation to heed any further advice. Yet the saints or some of them may prove of considerable assistance where they have left behind casual remarks and details about their own secret practices. When I use the word "saint," I am aware that the term is often restricted to those whose holy living has been officially approved by the Church. A great many of those whom I will mention have this official approbation and that helps. Yet the word "saint" was often used by St. Paul and others about devout and holy disciples, canonized or not. Clearly there have been many very holy people whose merits were duly recognized and honored without the official process of the Church. Let me write in this more general sense as does Professor E. Allison Peers in his delightful little book. This great Professor of Spanish, the translator of the works of St. Teresa, once delivered a series of radio lectures to South America, lectures which were later published in a book. He called his book *Behind That Wall* to preserve the image of a small Spanish village in which he had been staying, a village with a drab and untidy main street, flanked by a very dull and unattractive wall. Behind that wall, as he discovered when he was invited in, was a delightful Spanish patio and an exquisite Spanish home. In this typical and attractive setting, the Professor considers the lives of those, outwardly ordinary and unattractive, who in secret enjoyed a remarkable richness and peace. We are not obliged to copy such men, nor perhaps have we the strength to do so, but we might be able to profit from their experience. As Allison Peers puts it, "However difficult we may find it ourselves to live the interior life, however much our work or our troubles oppress us, however hard it may be to shake off the world and to concentrate on things that matter most, I think we ought sometimes to read books by people who have been more successful at this than ourselves, even if, in places, we are unable to follow them."

I must here heed the advice already quoted from Radhakrishnan and "not give supreme and sole importance to our specialty." Not all are attracted to saints or to history. One may pray very well without leaning on their example and some of their practices fill even their disciples with dismay. C. S. Lewis writing to Malcolm is glad that there is no process of canonization in the Church of England—"can you imagine a better hot-bed for yet more divisions between us?"—but he has to admit to a mounting interest in the doctrine of the Communion of Saints. "The consoling thing is that while Christendom is divided about the rationality and even the lawfulness of praying *to* the saints, we are all agreed about praying *with* them. *"With angels and archangels and all the company of heaven."* Will you believe it? It is only quite recently that I have made that quotation a part of my private prayers—I festoon it round 'Hallowed be Thy Name.' "

For myself, I must admit that I am not yet so exalted; consciously I do not pray to the saints or with the saints but they have always fascinated me as men. In youth I polished up my statues of my special favorites among them and even sneaked a relic of a saint to the bridge table in the vain hope of defeating my father at cards. Such superstitions discarded, I remember dividing up my favorite saints into three political parties, Labor, Liberal and Conservative. The idea was not a bad one for the saints enjoyed political views. As a teenager, my life was organized by a saintly cabinet. Eventually, "one puts away the things of a child," but with history as my professional subject, the draw of the saints has remained.

If we are to copy the saints in prayer, we must get to know them, not as plaster statues but as men. In a wide variety of situations they faced the same problems and attempted the same solutions as we do ourselves. No matter which the century or decade a similar brand of sincerity is required to face God in one's private room. Just as frozen fish needs resuscitation after a spell in the freezer, so the saints must be thawed out to become living, frightened, hopeful, eccentric men and women, struggling in a real environment. How some of them would have laughed to see their idealized image in stained glass. I have found it very rewarding to study the saints in their proper settings, for one then discovers with astonishment that they were not all that different from ourselves.

With just a few saints, Thomas More, Teresa, Cardinal Newman among them, we may still read the books which fashioned their youthful minds. Newman sets out his reading in his *Apologia,* More translated the works of Pico della Mirandola whom he then imitated, Teresa recommended a very heavy book for her old father who had asked her how to pray. Or one may study the handwriting of the saints and a handsome volume has been published with photographs of their letters and an analysis of their character based on their caligraphy.

By far the best way to learn about the saints is to visit the environs in which they lived and worked and prayed. At Ostia, one may stand before the lid of St. Monica's coffin to recall a bereavement which cost Augustine so many tears. Or you may follow Ignatius of Loyola from the room in his castle in which he read the gospel as a wounded soldier, to the cave at Manresa where he lived for a year, to the chapel where he pronounced his vows in Paris, finally to the small room in Rome and the iron balcony from which, as an old man, he viewed the stars. I have sat in the Curé's confessional at Ars, climbed the pulpit in Annecy Cathedral, knelt in St. Teresa's stall in Avila, stood by the Thames at Chelsea on the spot where Thomas More parted from his family. A pilgrimage with Bernadette proves most rewarding, starting in the Pyrenees by the river Gave at Lourdes and ending in the convent infirmary at Nevers. For me two historic sites were particularly moving, though thousands of miles and thousands of years apart. In 1959, I was taken to Midland, Ontario, even today a lonely and remote region, and to the remains of that little Indian village in which John de Brebeuf toiled and prayed and died. Far across the world near Jericho, I saw the long line of distant mountains from which Moses gazed at the Promised Land. Here for all of us is a fascinating form of field work combining a holiday with prayer, the only common factor in so many thousands of holy lives.

If we ask what we may learn from the saints about private prayer, I would have to suggest as an answer that absolute liberty of spirit would be the cardinal point. It is not only that they said this in so many words but, further, they showed it by example, each in secret following a personal line. Here one can do no more than generalize. On many subjects concerned with prayer, one saint or another offers us a useful comment or example and, after that, the testimony of almost all of them converges on two central points. Let us take some of the more immediate details first.

How many people ask about the length of prayer in private, and, significantly, the older saints provide no answer to this point. Private prayer cannot be measured by the clock. The more modern the saint, the more time-conscious, and no doubt the saints of the future will, before praying, check their clocks and watches by radio. The ancients with their sundials and hour glasses were more flexible. As far as I could find out, St. Ignatius was one of the first in the sixteenth century who measured meditation by the hour and this he did only in his *Spiritual Exercises,* a crash course, timed to last a month. Elsewhere even Ignatius is vague—"I will stand for the space of a Pater Noster," a measurement which could mean anything. Paul Giustiniani, a contemporary of Ignatius, in writing rules of life for his hermits, pins them down for half an hour a day: "Each one will choose the time best suited to him when he will remain motionless in mental prayer for at least half an hour, either all at once or divided into shorter periods." Among the moderns, Déchanet is equally vague about time in his *Christian Yoga,* stressing the need for physical and mental preparation before the moment of prayer is reached: "The contemplative phase in daily meditation may last ten or fifteen minutes, but its duration in fact varies a great deal and how long it lasts is, moreover, of relatively little importance." On the question of time in private prayer, I have followed Sir Thomas More for years. In his translation of the works of Pico della Mirandola, young More gives us this version of the Italian scholar's thought: "Nor care I how long or how short thy prayer be but how effectual, how ardent . . . let no day pass then but thou, once at leastwise, present thyself to God in prayer and falling down before him flat to the ground."

Posture in Prayer

As with time, so with posture, the saints showed themselves more flexible, less inhibited than many of us are today. They allowed themselves almost every posture down to the elaborate yoga exercises so well described by Déchanet. At Ostia, Augustine was standing by a window when he and his saintly mother were swept away in ecstasy. One also finds reference in Augustine to prayer with the forehead on the ground. In every instance, Ignatius of Loyola is the most precise and he sets out a variety of postures in his *Spiritual Exercises,* postures which he had almost certainly tried out for himself. He writes, "The fourth note is to enter into contemplation at one time kneeling, at another prostrate on the earth or stretched on the ground with my face upwards; now seated, now standing, ever intent on seeking that which I desire. Two things are to be noted: first, if kneeling or prostrate I find that which I want, I will not try any other position; secondly, that in the point in which I shall find what I desire, there will I rest without being anxious to proceed to another until I have satisfied myself."

Kneeling at prayer was the common posture in the Victorian era and was considered apt on certain occasions, especially to express sorrow and contrition in every age. Among moderns, C. S. Lewis favors kneeling, "for the body ought to pray as well as the soul." Richard Rolle, the cheery old hermit of Hampole, for some curious reason insisted on sitting for prayer. "I have loved to sit," he says, "for no penance nor for any fantasy that I would have men speak of me, nor for any such thing, but only because I knew that I loved God more and lasted longer within the comfort of love than going on standing or kneeling. For by sitting am I in most rest and my heart most upward."

On one point alone do the saints agree in the matter of posture, that we should not fidget but assume that position that induces peace, rest and tranquility. We saw how Ignatius stresses this and how Giustiniani expects his hermits to be motionless. Yoga asks no less. Teresa, writing about the prayer of quiet, puts the position well: "It seems to her that she wants nothing more; the faculties which are at rest would like always to remain still, for the least of their movements is able to trouble or to prevent her love. Those who are in this prayer wish their bodies to remain motionless, for it seems to them that, at the least movement, they will lose this sweet peace."

The Place of Prayer

On this subject, too, the saints differ widely, save in their insistence on solitude. Though, from time to time, they would pray in a crowd or with their community or on a journey, such prayer was accidental and no substitute for prayer in their rooms. As has already been noted, Thomas More took Christ literally and liked praying in a room. His spirit was Carthusian and the sense of confinement helped to vitalize his solitude. When held as a prisoner in the Tower of London, he was said to have been the most contented prisoner seen in that grim place. When he was at the peak of his career, More constructed a special building to which he could retire for prayer. As his son-in-law explains, "And because he was desirous for godly purposes sometimes to be solitary and sequester himself from worldly company, a good distance from his mansion house builded he a place called the New Building, wherein there was a chapel, a library and a gallery; in which, as his use was upon other days to occupy himself in prayer and study together, so on the Friday there usually he continued from morning till evening, spending his time only in devout prayer and spiritual exercises."

Provided that they were alone and undistracted, the majority of saints and prayerful people were less particular than Sir Thomas More. They prayed where they liked. Henry Suso, the medieval mystic returned to the Convent Church after breakfast, when it would be empty, and sat "in the last stall on the prior's side."

Ignatius, when living in his cave outside Barcelona, walked four miles to the parish Church of Manresa "always possessing his soul in tranquillity." C. S. Lewis was far less happy about churches. "I have had bad luck with churches," he writes, "no sooner do I enter one and compose my mind than one or other of two things happen, either someone starts practising the organ or else, with resolute tread, there appears from nowhere a pious woman in elastic-sided boots carrying mop and bucket, etc." Lewis, when busy, found it easier to pray in a crowded train on the way to a lecture than postpone his prayer until he was sleepy late in the day. "On other and slightly less crowded days, a bench in the park or a back street where one can pace up and down will do."

Many saints, St. Francis of Assisi among them, liked to pray in the open air. St. Gertrude went to the convent courtyard and prayed sitting by a fountain. Simone Weil as already noted, recited the Our Father in Greek as she tended the Portuguese vines. Dom John Chapman, living on Caldey Island, spent two hours in a cleft of a rock "where I could fancy that I was the last man." In the case of St. Ignatius of Loyola, we meet a curious incident in which the saint found that he was making a mistake in his prayers. In those first strenuous days after his conversion, Ignatius began praying immediately he went to bed at night. So overwhelming were his thoughts that his all too short hours of sleep were curtailed. He took advice about this and following the direction of another, stopped himself if he found himself starting to pray at night.

We find, then, among the saints a delightful liberty of spirit as to time, place and posture in their secret prayer. There was with them no conscious imitation or conventional pattern, prior to the formalism of Victorian times. We must remember that a great many saints were occupied with the liturgy and with choir so that private prayer was a relaxation, an act of friendship, the culmination of the monastic day.

Differing as they did in temperament and background, the saints were by no means uniform in prayer. But it became clear to me that they agreed on certain principles which we, too, might find helpful and on one painful situation which we for certain must face. Let us take this first, briefly, for we are bound in one way or another to taste the tedium of prayer.

The Tedium of Prayer

I could find among the saints and masters of prayer no effort to disguise the tedium of prayer. At one stage or another, all save Brother Lawrence endured a period of boredom and frustration, often stemming from loneliness. Brother Lawrence deserves special mention, a special paragraph for an unusual type. This cheerful, simple man, apparently without any troubles, was to exercise a considerable influence in seventeenth-century France. Once a footman to an aristocratic family, our hero was dismissed, to use his own description, "as a great awkward fellow who broke everything." William James would, I think, have classed Brother Lawrence among the "once born." Those who share his temperament may forge ahead cheerfully. Brother Lawrence certainly did. Describing his life as a cook in the Carmelite kitchen, he revealed a simplicity which would win all hearts. "In the noise and clutter of my kitchen, while several people are, at the same time, calling for different things, I possess God in great tranquillity as if I were upon my knees before the Blessed Sacrament." Brother Lawrence seems from the distance of three hundred years to provide for us one lesson, that a man may attain to a high gift of prayer without enduring any dark night of the soul.

Few other holy people enjoy such a temperament. For many there was some suffering in prayer, stemming from a variety of causes too complex for discussion here. Thus, for those saints who experienced a sudden conversion, there were the pains normal to any violent adjustment, the longing to abandon so much tedious effort and to return to a previous complacency. Such frustration did not derive from prayer and in the end was mastered by it, but it deserves a passing mention as an experience commonly linked with the life of prayer. Augustine's long and arduous struggle towards liberation, set out in his *Confessions,* well illustrates the point. Other saints with Ignatius of Loyola suffered from an excess of fervor after their conversion, weakened their physical stamina through indiscretion and, for a time, paid for this a painful price. One hesitates to apply the fashionable word "neurotic" to holy people but symptoms which today would be judged neurotic appear not infrequently in prayerful lives. The early chapters of St. Teresa's *Autobiography* may serve as an illustration, also the account given by Ignatius of his year in the Manresa cave. Ignatius, as he tells us, was tempted to suicide. Francis de Sales endured a period of intense depression in his student days. William James in his *Varieties* was particularly severe on St. Margaret Mary and other writers have, for much the same reasons, criticized the spirituality of St. Thérèse de Lisieux. Such criticisms, which thirty years ago were regarded as a prejudiced attack on the Christian Churches, may now be accepted more tolerantly. In the lives of many great men and women, a struggle against neurosis and instability is observable and religious people, because of the profundity of their desires and ambitions, are in a special way vulnerable. George Fox, Bunyan, Robert Louis Stevenson, Luther and Wesley join Teresa of Avila, Ignatius of Loyola and other saints in such initial suffering. In all these cases, private prayer, faithfully maintained, finally produced an impressive form of peace and stability.

When writing about tedium in prayer, I would not wish to include such mental and spiritual upheavals as may be endured by people of a certain temperament. Nor need we involve ourselves in those further spiritual sufferings known to those who seek to free themselves utterly from the self-centeredness of sense. One school of prayer, now inevitably identified with St. John of the Cross, made so much of the dark night of the soul and of the senses, that it has become fashionable to suppose that all true contemplatives must endure such loss. The lives of the saints, taken as a whole, do not appear to confirm this gloomy view. There will be a certain type of saint, as there will also be a certain type of poet or musician, whose genius may express itself in deep, internal anguish, verging on morbidity. Among certain spiritual writers such darkness is viewed as a necessity. Dom John Chapman writes in a letter, "Do not worry about your mental balance. Both Father Baker and Père de Caussade think that we may easily have to make an act of abandon that we are willing to go mad if God wishes; only it comes to nothing and it does not happen. It is a very painful state to be in; but so much the better." A little more about this curious attitude may be added later on.

For myself, I am able to appreciate the mental suffering of certain holy people without accepting the theory that such pain in prayer is inevitable. Some of it is self-induced. People who pray in secret need not suffer, though prayer by sharpening our awareness may well make us more sensitive. For some unexplained reason, we all tend to associate being sensitive with suffering, forgetting the extreme joy that sensitivity also brings. When Christ spoke about prayer in the Sermon on the Mount, he made no mention of suffering but stated expressly that if we prayed in secret our Father would reward us. Taking the literature about prayer as a whole, we must, I think, reach the honest judgment that prayer in private brings an enduring happiness and peace.

Whether we suffer or not, few of us will escape the sheer tedium which prayer in private brings. As the saints describe it, it appears as a mixture of monotony, weariness and frustration, so often observable in "shut-ins." The old, the sick, the bereaved taste such bitterness and have to learn to live with it. How often have I witnessed such sudden spells of boredom and exhaustion which end in tears of sheer weariness. Those of you who have been sick will have experienced that fearsome dilemma of the choice between your own wretched company or the fatigue of sweating through another unattractive book. Now the man of prayer, going to his private room, freely accepts such a tedium which he could so easily avoid. Off he goes, day after day, in the hope of enjoying an inner satisfaction, previously experienced. The saints all knew and we, too, have to discover that a sensitive awareness of God's presence is always possible but cannot be induced. Not being a poet, musician, artist, I am able only to imagine the long frustrations of a thwarted genius. With writers I am more familiar and have witnessed the weeks and months of irritation and despondence when ideas are stillborn and words refuse to fit into place. Tedium for the man of prayer may be compared to this.

Prayer in private is an art and the saints along with other artists anticipated tedium and learned to live with it. Certainly they made no attempt to disguise the unpalatable fact. Teresa of Avila seems to derive some pleasure in describing her many years of weariness. Paul Giustiniani writes in detail about the problem and seeks to explain why it should be that an exercise which proves overwhelmingly satisfying and rewarding looks so unattractive each day as one retires alone. Our hermit gladly admits to the constant temptation to postpone his prayer. He puts the blame on his body and compares his efforts in prayer to the exhaustion of a mountain climber who suffers so much with each step upwards but finds no trouble when travelling down hill. If one saint may be quoted for all, I would select a passage from St. Peter of Alcantara, St. Teresa's friend. As St. Peter sees it, the very glory of God's majesty, the very lowliness of our situation, account for "the many times that we are kept waiting, pacing up and down like sentries at the palace gate." I find this simile refreshing and the passage which follows it: "If you have not adored Our Lord with such fervor of devotion as you had wished, it is enough that you have adored him in spirit and truth which is the way he desires. Believe me, this is certainly the most perilous spot in the journey and the place that tests those who are really devout. If you come well out of this, all the rest will go prosperously."

The Presence of God

The saints who have described their prayer, invariably begin with a common exercise; in one form or another they put themselves into the presence of God. *"Mettez-vous en la presence de Dieu,"* writes St. Francis de Sales before every meditation, and C. S. Lewis wonders "how many different mental operations have been carried out in intended obedience to that?" For most saints this exercise is the beginning of prayer but not, of course, for Brother Lawrence who once admitted that all his prayers and the whole of his prayers added up to "nothing else but a sense of the presence of God." Professor Allison Peers sees Brother Lawrence as the initiator of a new style of prayer in seventeenth-century France.

On all matters of prayer, Ignatius of Loyola, the Basque nobleman and soldier, is the most exact: "I will stand for the space of a Pater Noster, one or two paces from the place in which I am about to contemplate or meditate, and, with mind raised on high, consider how God, Our Lord, sees me and I will make an act of reverence and humiliation." Other saints are not quite so precise. Yet they all insist that prayer in secret must be formal at least at the start. It is not just sufficient to read a book or to walk about mooning, a temptation which at times may prove exceptionally strong. A great many of our prayers are damaged because we cannot bring ourselves to start.

More may be added to this subject in the final chapter but here it will be sufficient to emphasize the importance of beginning well. Christ's words surely imply some form of confrontation between ourselves and the invisible God. *"But when you pray, go into a room by yourself, shut the door and pray to your Father who is there in the secret place; and your Father who sees what is secret will reward you."* It was Simone Weil's contention that original sin still shows itself in a dread of such a confrontation, a dread first expressed by Adam and Eve when God came to walk in the Garden of Eden at eventide. The urge to escape may be great and the alternative confrontation so alarming that many will snatch at any excuse not to begin.

In an earlier chapter, I quoted Simone Weil about attention and I would like to repeat here that one sentence which seems to serve as a key for private prayer. "Prayer," she wrote, "consists of attention. It is the orientation of all the attention of which the soul is capable towards God." Her whole essay expands this theme and shows how our way of life, our manual work, our reading, our use of leisure may play a significant part in our power of attention when we retire to our rooms to pray. After all, it was entirely through inattention that those foolish bridesmaids in the gospel missed the wedding feast.

Certain saints on certain occasions showed a startling power of attention when putting themselves in the presence of God. Such an attention was without doubt caused by a Divine insight which enabled them to become aware of the presence of God. Yet, however commanding the Divine intervention, part of this mystical experience derived from a life of attention and awareness on the part of the recipient. Among the bird-watchers on the Isles of Scilly those see more who have by practice trained themselves to look. The most startling expression of this gift I found many years ago in the life of St. Aloysius Gonzaga, the sixteenth-century Italian prince who abandoned great worldly possessions to become a Jesuit. I have never been able to find the reference again. According to the story, the young Italian once said that he could pray for hours without any distraction and this assertion was challenged by his friends. Among these was an old priest, later canonized as St. Robert Bellarmine, who maintained that prayer without distraction for so long a spell was impossible. Aloysius then came out with his remarkable statement: "If you know that God is in the room, it would be a miracle to have a distraction!" A similar absorption is seen in the prayer of Bernadette at the Lourdes grotto and in the life of that unusual boy, St. Dominic Savio, in Turin. When Christ at the age of twelve was lost in the Temple, I suspect that a similar but stronger attraction lay behind the event. Maybe such intensity of attention goes with youth.

A great many older saints also experienced this mystical attention but with them it was more sporadic and not continuous. At least they never presumed to count on it. If they were aware of

God's presence in their secret place, then their prayer needed no further effort or ingenuity. Provided that we accept the fact that such attention, divinely inspired, is possible at any moment, we may for the moment leave the point.

Generalizations are dangerous but to judge from their writings, no saints, other than Brother Lawrence, enjoyed an uninterrupted sense of God's presence continuously. Like ourselves they had spells—even long spells—of dryness and sensible apathy. The fact of God's presence they accepted and the satisfaction of adoring God as one of his creatures drew them to pray despite the ennui. After all, mothers, doctors, nurses show their affection to their children or to their patients by their fidelity of service even when feeling flat. To stimulate their attention on less easy occasions, the saints used many devices to help themselves. Hence we come across frequent references to images and statues, so placed to hold the attention, to remind the prayerful person of the presence of God. Both St. Teresa and St. Thomas More found sensible assistance in such objects and the Greek and Russian saints made use of ikons as an aid to prayer. One Russian bishop informed me that he always put his ikon at eye level and looked into the eyes of the figure as a form of prayer. He prayed thus by glances and, while not for a moment worshipping an image, took it as a rendezvous with God. Archbishop Goodier of Bombay, when very tired, sat at a desk with a piece of paper before him on which he made a tick after he had recited the Glory be to the Father, Son and Holy Spirit. The one essential in prayer, as the saints describe it, is to start formally with the recollection that one is in the presence of God. Such an operation may absorb hours on certain happy occasions or it may end in a second according to our age, temperament, situation, health or mood.

On the use of images to focus attention, it may help to note the practice used by the Hindu. In Sacred Yoga, a most helpful device is used. Father Déchanet describes it thus: "The Guru or spiritual director will choose for his disciple the *place* of concentration as well as the *subject,* or rather the *object* of meditation. This object will initially be a physical object, a tree, some kind of fruit, a landscape, or else the representation of a chosen deity in the form of a sculpture or picture. This picture or object or shape is placed in the area concentrated on, such as the forehead or the heart and visualized as being there. It must appear there and one must see it clearly in all its details; one must be aware of its presence as of the presence of a real, living thing. The whole affair, in fact, consists in stabilizing and fixing the inner vision, the mind. In order that it may concentrate actively and not get snatched away even for a moment by any distraction, it is forced to imagine or picture to itself, in full detail, some shape already perceived by the senses. This material image is an aid called in merely to be dismissed later on. Soon enough, the mind will call up and vizualize, at any given point, without external aids, the image of God."

Where some saints used such images and pictures, others having called to mind God's presence, fell back on meditative reading with many pauses or on the use of a few words. As we have seen, the author of *The Cloud of Unknowing* suggests two simple words, "sin" and "God." The favorite phrase of St. Francis of Assisi was "My God and my All." Alphonsus Rodriguez, a widower who became a Jesuit brother, describes his method thus: "This person placed himself in the presence of God, saying to him lovingly with heart and mouth, 'Lord, let me know thee, let me know myself,' and at once he was lifted up, above all created things, and he found himself, as it were, in another region, alone with God."

To this use of words, other saints also added gestures to bring home to themselves the presence of God in the room. The classic example of this, written in the third person, was penned in the Tower of London not long before his execution by Sir Thomas More. More often wrote in the third person about himself. We cannot doubt that this was how More had often prayed and the passage gains in content from the fact that the man praying was a scholar and a former Lord Chancellor of England, a man with a European reputation and the author of *Utopia*. "Let him also choose himself some secret solitary place in his own house, as far from noise and company as he conveniently can and, thither, let him sometimes secretly resort alone, imagining as one going out of this world even straight unto the giving up his reckoning unto God of his sinful living. Then let him there, before an altar or some pitiful image of Christ's most bitter passion (the beholding whereof may put him in remembrance of the thing and move him to devout compassion), kneel down or fall prostrate, as it were at the feet of Almighty God, verily believing him to be there, invisibly present, as without doubt he is. There let him open his heart to God and confess his faults, such as he can call to mind and pray God for forgiveness. Let him call to remembrance the benefits that God has given to him, either in general among other men or privately to himself and give him humble, hearty thanks thereof."

Lord, Teach Us to Pray

From the writing of the saints about prayer we learn two common lessons, first to put ourselves formally in the presence of God at the beginning; secondly, not to forget to ask God or His Holy Spirit to help us in our prayer. There could, I think, be no greater error in prayer than the frequent assumption that we are able to pray adequately without Divine aid. A curious type of

Pelagianism persuades many that they can by personal effort attain to sanctity. Here is the error behind all Puritanism and false righteousness. Hence the saints make much of their inadequacy and stress the need for humble supplication that God will aid them in their prayer.

If this essential requirement must be fulfilled in ordinary prayer, how much more vital it is in that prayer which is supernatural and relies on Divine cooperation for its result. All those more intimate forms of prayer which Teresa would recognize as advances on the Prayer of Quiet cannot be induced by any effort on our part. She says as much over and over again. She tells us that we can do no more than prepare and dispose ourselves for such gifts and beg God to favor us in this way. For in Christ's injunctions about secret prayer, a secret dialogue is implied. We in secret adore God, express our love, our sorrow, our desires and he who is able to assess such aspirations made in secret, rewards them by his gifts. Two make a friendship, make a conversation, make a prayer. Simone Weil as usual sums up the message of the saints: "It is God alone who comes down and possesses the soul but desire alone draws God down. He only comes to those who ask him to come; and he cannot refuse to come to those who implore him long, often and ardently."

8.

Imaginative Contemplation

It is not easy to explain why, when we want to pay attention, we immediately brace our muscles to take the strain. Do we truly believe that our muscles when taut will the better help our brain? No doubt we thus react through force of habit, a very bad habit widely adopted in the West.

If, as a schoolmaster, I say to my class, "Now I want you all to pay great attention," they will immediately tighten up their muscles as though preparing for a race. They will haul themselves up in their chairs, throw back their shoulders, contract their brows, hold their breath, pull earnest faces as though such bodily contortions will help them to concentrate. This in fact is precisely what they are doing, concentrating on their muscles and paying small attention to the point that I am trying to explain. In a very short time they will be restless and exhausted and quite unable to repeat a word of what I have said. A boy, lounging on a sofa relaxed, is able to give his full attention to the novel that he is reading because his muscles are relaxed.

Adults are probably worse than children in this tightening of the muscles under the false impression that they are thus giving full attention to the task in hand. For some curious reason we were never taught that muscular relaxation fosters true attention, permitting the mind to hold itself in suspension before turning itself wholly to the subject about which it wishes to think. We should tighten our muscles only when we want our body to react to a situation, to run, sit, stand, avoid a danger, side-step an accident. When the mind only is involved in paying attention, the body is best out of the way. We speak about "putting our mind" to a task but such an operation needs no muscles and is best achieved when the body is relaxed.

Muscular relaxation is, then, a matter of considerable importance in the sphere of thought. As prayer is linked to thought and, as St. Paul says, is an involvement of mind and spirit, it may be considerably affected by our bodily attitudes. Those who practice yoga discover with amazement how breath control and muscular relaxation play a significant part both in thought and in prayer. The yoga exercises are effective in teaching us how to relax our bodies and many who have small use for prayer or religion take up yoga simply to acquire peace. In this limited sphere of muscular control it proves highly rewarding, though much weakened and diluted when thus divorced from its proper end. Used to stabilize the mind, its results are far-reaching but such mental control is in sacred yoga no more than a means to an end. The end for yoga is prayer and the journey from the self-conscious to the cosmic conscious and so to consciousness of the Divine.

In my field work on the Isles of Scilly, I have read much about yoga and in a limited way practiced it. Further, I have been fortunate in that two or three friends are much experienced in the art. Yet I cannot call myself a disciple for the simple reason that I came, by accident, upon a more amateur and simpler form of yoga twenty-five years ago. I say "by accident" because I was not searching for any help in prayer when I went to Glasgow in 1945. Indeed, I was lecturing and giving retreats and preached at the great Church on Garnethill for a momentous occasion, the victory over Japan. What I had not grasped at the time was the strain under which we had all been living during the years of the Second World War. What with monotonous food, bad nights, V bombs and blackouts, the whole of Europe was exhausted and we were lucky in Britain to be as cheerful and healthy as we were. This autobiographical fact is worth recalling, for very few tired people recognize their symptoms and hence rarely seek the right cure. Luckily for me, I came upon a most unusual and sympathetic person, Sister Marie Hilda, in the Child Guidance Clinic which she had just established at Dowanhill. She, it was, who spoke to me about muscular relaxation and gave me the book about it which I have before me now. Inside the cover is written, "Glasgow Educational Department, Not To Be Taken Away."

Relaxation in Everyday Life was written by two doctors, E. J. Boome and M. A. Richardson. It was published in 1931. Since that date many similar books have appeared covering the same subject and I would not claim for my two doctors any very original thinking, though I owe to both of them an impressive debt. It was part of Sister Marie Hilda's approach to steer clear of books by her fellow psychiatrists. She loved her profession but reckoned that the constant dealing with true mental illness made many psychiatrists too involved and complicated and that the art of relaxation is simple and natural. Animals and children relax by instinct and adults need only to be re-educated in a skill that they had thrown away. How wise was the line she took. The fact that this therapy was normal and natural removed any sort of panic and my two doctors wrote in simple English without involving me in dream interpretations, the probing of the unconscious, the jargon given to the world by Freud. Their skill was partly in their style of writing, for they not only persuaded me to read about muscular relaxation but to practice it. A self-important man of forty needs much cunning persuasion before he is ready to stretch out on the ground.

Let me quote the opening lines of the first exercise that Drs.

106

Boome and Richardson persuaded me to do. "Lie flat on the back with the body in a straight line on a comfortable flat surface—a bed that sags in the middle is not advisable, nor a sofa that does not allow sufficient space or support. Choose the floor rather than either of these.

"Allow the bed or floor to receive your full weight. This sounds simple enough but it is only after repeated practice has brought you to within measurable distance of carry out that simple order that you will realize how far short you were on that first occasion of yielding your *full weight*."

If space permitted, I would quote more of this admirable book. Drs. Boome and Richardson proved right and it took me at least three months of practice before I could trust the floor to receive my full weight. As the weeks went by, I began to master the basic lessons, how to relax the chest, how to breathe deeply, how to surrender to mental content. Slowly but surely one moved to that half-way stage between consciousness and sleep. At times, sleep would come first but rarely for more than a few minutes, after which one entered into an alert but restful mood. It was a new and extraordinary experience to lie still for an hour with no desire to move. Real attention became possible and was unusually satisfying and with this enhanced faculty one could drink in one *object* or *subject* without a distraction of any kind. One peculiar feature of the exercise was the way it would end. After the first few weeks, it became quite unnecessary to fix any limits, to say to oneself, "You must lie there for half an hour whether you like it or not." Some mechanism inside the human machine seemed to indicate the moment when the therapy was over and one had relaxed enough. Yet there were occasions when it became abundantly clear on standing that the session had ended too quickly and that one needed to get down on the floor again.

As you may have guessed, my authors were not only concerned

with muscular relaxation and, after a time, they began to suggest simple, imaginative pictures which would quieten the mind. Thus they proposed for my attention "a restful landscape, a calm sea, a range of mountains or the sky." By Chapter Seven such imaginative scenes had assumed a more positive form of guidance and there was one particular sentence which attracted me. Drs. Boome and Richardson added an aside for the sake of younger therapists or doctors: "The type of suggestion which will help the patient to deeper relaxation will naturally be adapted to his individual needs by the therapist in charge of the case." Happily, I had no therapist, only a borrowed book. This book, like its mental images, was altering slightly, showing how relaxation could help cases of epilepsy, asthma, stammering, exophthalmic goitre, insomnia, none of which maladies, fortunately, were troubling me.

I parted company with Doctors Richardson and Boome after they had mentioned these still deeper forms of relaxation and the careful choice of subjects which might trigger these off. As I knew my own case, I could guess the topics which would be most restful to me. So, lying on the floor relaxed and no longer in the least shy about this undignified posture, I came to follow Christ through the gospel scenes. The operation made me smile for I was back to square one, back to the days of my youth when I entered the Jesuit noviciate, for here was the method of prayer so dear to St. Ignatius, St. Francis de Sales and others who were still in fashion when I was young.

I could spot the obvious difference of approach after twenty years. As a young man I had been earnest, anxious, ambitious, determined to master prayer, easily moved by my emotions, absolutely confident. Now I was forty, much less sure, much more peaceful and passive, much more relaxed after so many months with Drs. Richardson and Boome. Sometimes I now wonder why relaxation was never mentioned in the nineteen twenties, nor was this therapy to my knowledge ever linked with prayer. In vain I have searched many books by great Western writers to find so much as a hint of the advantages of praying relaxed on the ground. Yet Ignatius of Loyola and the other Renaissance masters may well have known the secret four centuries ahead of Drs. Richardson and Boome. In a passage already quoted, Ignatius advises his clients to pray stretched out upon the ground. And in a letter which he wrote from Venice in 1536, he seems to be leading up to a prayer of relaxation: "All meditations where the understanding works, fatigue the body. There are other meditations, equally in the order of God, which are restful, full of peace for the understanding, without labor for the interior faculties of the soul and which are performed without either physical or interior effort."

Those familiar with yoga will recognize in my accidental method much that is borrowed from Hindu lore. Others may have hit upon other systems, more scientific and up-to-date than mine. The one essential for all of us who pray in secret is muscular relaxation with its unique value not only on the physical and mental levels but also on the plane of secret prayer. Its effectiveness in prayer derives from the swift increase of quiet attention and alertness which it unfailingly provides. I am unable to explain this result, part of which is the silencing of distractions, part the easy acceptance of long pauses without embarrassment. Distractions seem to lose their malice for one who is lying down. Relaxation permits one to pay full attention and seems to supply a control of the imagination which is invaluable in prayer.

There are those who throw up their hands in horror at the very mention of imagination in the field of prayer. The validity of such a posture and such condemnation may be considered briefly later in this book. Once I would have accepted censure for imaginative praying but not now. As absolute liberty of spirit is the right of every prayerful person, those with the gift of imagination have both the right and duty to harness such a talent and use it in their search for God. A great many saints were imaginative in their prayers and who can blame them, when modern psychiatrists are employing imaginative suggestions to their patients as a means of inducing stability and peace. Christ himself made no direct mention of imagination but in his parables gave us some of the greatest imaginative pictures in the world. He moved easily from the visible to the invisible by means of simile.

On this subject of imagination in prayer, C. S. Lewis, unlike other contemporary writers, takes up a sane and well-balanced attitude. Writing of St. Paul's vivid phrase "meeting God face to face," the Oxford professor defends the expression while exposing a popular deceit. "This talk of 'meeting' is no doubt anthropomorphic; as if God and I could be face to face like two fellow creatures when in reality He is above me and within me and below me and about me. That is why it must be balanced by all manner of metaphysical and theological abstractions. But never here or anywhere else let us think that while anthropomorphic images are a concession to our weakness, the abstractions are the literal truth. Both are equally concessions; each singly misleading and the two together mutually corrective. Unless you sit to it very lightly, continually murmuring, 'Not thus, not thus, neither is this Thou,' the abstraction is fatal. It will make the life of lives inanimate and the love of loves impersonal. The naïf image is mischievous chiefly in so far as it holds unbelievers from conversion. It does believers, even in its crudest form, no harm. What soul ever perished for believing that God the Father really has a beard?"

Whatever we may think of the pictures and images of God—

God himself strictly forbade them in the Old Testament, we have no honest grounds for condemning an imaginative approach to Christ. If we are prepared to watch Julius Caesar on the stage or the Hollywood epics from Spartacus to Cromwell, why should we baulk at imagining Christ? True, we have no record of Christ's looks and to this extent may be inaccurate in our presentation, but inaccuracies are not always harmful and have played a significant part both in art and in history. I was puzzled to find that C. S. Lewis, who makes so much of the imagery of Milton and Dante, can write, "We no longer, as St. Ignatius could, believingly introduce the clothes, furniture and utensils of our age into ancient Palestine."

The danger of picturing Christ in prayer will not derive from seeing him at Cana with a modern wine glass or a Renaissance cup. False emotions and an excess of sentimentality prove far more enervating and these may be corrected by careful attention to the gospel text. The four evangelists keep well clear of the "glorious technicolor" approach. For twelve hundred years, the humanity of Christ was honored and treasured but kept free from the sensual imagery which would later evolve around his cult. In the centuries following St. Francis of Assisi, we note an ever mounting attraction towards Christ's physical features and underlying humanity. Such a development in the later Middle Ages is observable in theology, painting, preaching, sculpture and every form of pious art. The influence of St. Francis on our Western culture is paramount. That great devotion, much generosity, new patterns of holiness derived from all this need not be doubted, but with it went, in some pious quarters, much that was maudlin and sensuous. Along with William James, we too may suffer goose-flesh when reading some of the more amorous outpourings of the medieval mystics, some of them saints. Liberty of spirit in private prayer must prevent us from con-

111

demning so emotional an approach but we need not accept it for ourselves. The contemplation of Christ's human life by means of imagination and mental pictures for many years suited me. The justification for such a method of prayer may perhaps be found in the number of tough and unemotional saints who used it and in the fact that it exactly fits the requirements for relaxation set out by Drs. Richardson and Boome.

The arguments for this method of prayer were for me considerably strengthened after I had practiced relaxation and read some of the suggestions made by my two doctors for achieving it. Thus I read in their book: "Every action we perform has to be mentally conceived before it can be carried out. The interval between its conception and performance is so short that we are very seldom consciously aware of the process. But the performance will be good or bad according to the habitual or momentary picture that precedes it. Why do you continually serve double faults at tennis now? You never did so until recently. Simply because you have formed the habit of 'seeing' yourself serving double faults. It probably started by an interference with exact coordination of brain and muscle, due perhaps to some slight muscular maladjustment, so slight as to be entirely overlooked. A day or two of faulty play as a result of this, set up the fear of repeating the bad performance, by which time you saw yourself serving badly and proceeded to do so. This type of incorrect imagery is quite easy to put right by practising your tennis service mentally during relaxation. The trouble has not been going on for long and is in no sense deep-seated. Very little practice should put it right. Having corrected your mental picture of the act, carry it about with you as you might a photograph. Take it out and look at it frequently between practices. When you come to the actual performance, look quietly at your mental picture and proceed to carry it out. If you do not succeed during the first game, do not be discouraged. It will only mean that you have not trusted yourself sufficiently and have allowed the old picture to intrude. You will be serving quite well again before the end of the set." Need I add that Drs. Richardson and Boome do not limit this therapy to tennis; in almost every field of activity they offer marked improvement to those who form happy and successful mental pictures while lying relaxed on the ground.

Some readers may wonder why, in a book about private prayer, I should thus turn to the uses of imagination on the tennis court. Is so long a diversion justified? In my field work on prayer, I could not see this topic as a diversion, for it lies at the very center of that method of contemplation so much favored by Renaissance saints. Nor is the subject irrelevant today, for the methods advocated by Drs. Richardson and Boome in the nineteen thirties have received powerful confirmation in our own day. Maxwell Maltz in his *Psycho-Cybernetics* popularized this line of positive thinking throughout the English-speaking world. This exuberant book carries such enticing headings as "Use Mental Pictures to Get a Better Job," "A Concert Pianist Practises in His Head," "How Imagination Practice Won a Chess Championship." A method that was first used to restore confidence after plastic surgery was now to become the rosy path to every success. Maltz sets out his remedy thus: "Get a New Mental Picture of Yourself. Science has now confirmed what philosophers, mystics and other intuitive people have long declared; every human being has been literally 'engineered for success' by his creator. Every human being has access to a power greater than himself."

Here we have scope for extensive field work, though I doubt if the God of heaven will provide supernatural assistance to prevent you from serving double faults. The value of auto-suggestion is undoubted and its application in one form or another as old as the hills. Dr. Maltz restates in colorful language the theory taught in my boyhood by the Frenchman, Dr. Coué: "Every day and in every way I get better and better." The method works up to a point and those who picture success in their imagination may well enjoy a success story in real life. There is, however, a flaw, one which is able to vitiate the whole process and bring nothing but disaster in its train. Not once but many times I have had to deal with those who have upset their mental balance by artificial and false imaginings of their own non-existent excellence. How many people in their effort to supply for lack of confidence manufacture an odious form of aggressiveness?

For some time, I had been seeking to qualify the promises contained in *Psycho-Cybernetics* and to point to the kind of imaginative weakness which could wreck the picture of success. Maybe Albert Speer, in his *Inside the Third Reich,* summing up the story of Hitler, comes near to the warning that I would like to underline. "In a sense he was worshipping himself. He was for ever holding up to himself a mirror in which he not only saw himself but also the confirmation of his mission by divine providence. His religion was based on 'the lucky break' which must necessarily come his way; his method was to reinforce himself by auto-suggestion . . . if there was any fundamental insanity in Hitler it was his unshakable belief in his 'lucky star.' He was by nature a religious man but his capacity for belief had been perverted into belief in himself."

Whatever our attitude to psycho-cybernetics and to success in this world, few Christians can apply the method to the next. We are too much aware of our personal back-sliding and sinfulness. For very good reasons, most men in secret are humble and inadequate. When Christ proposes that we pray in secret, he invites us to meet his Father when at our lowest ebb. Not only are we low but the sense of past failure makes it virtually impossible to produce a successful spiritual image of ourselves. I would like to suggest that in certain epochs, especially the Victorian, a spiritual form of psycho-cybernetics gave out a false, imaginative picture of holiness. Just as, in the social field, the image of a gentleman produced an artificial snobbery, so in religious matters was concocted a stilted form of sanctity. The most casual survey of Victorian stained-glass windows will illustrate this point. Whoever saw in glass a stout saint, a nervy saint or a saint who laughed? One came to presume that a saint never had a drink though the bulk of saints came from the warmer climates and grew up on wine. Saints were supposed not to enjoy their food, they had to look grave and godly in their hairshirts, itching unendingly. Sanctity in stained-glass seemed to imply many hours of prayer a day on a mahogany prie-dieu, so favored a feature of the Victorian pious world. Anyone who set out to become a saint through such mental images would end up with the psychiatrist.

The only safe and sure way of composing the right mental pictures of sanctity in a human setting is to contemplate the gospel scenes. The method which drew its spirit from St. Francis of Assisi was popular with spiritual writers at the start of the sixteenth century. Many saints used the word "contemplation" for this imaginative form of prayer. Here was the source of some confusion, for contemplation was normally reserved for that style of prayer which derived purely from the intervention of God. Imaginative prayer would not be regarded as contemplation by such saints as St. John of the Cross. Yet, in a true sense, one was contemplating the scenes of the gospel and could pass if God willed it to the deepest forms of mystical prayer.

For me, this simple form of prayer, which I had known since

boyhood, came to life only when Drs. Richardson and Boome had me relaxed and prostrate on the ground. Lying thus relaxed, the patient needs to think of something or, better, to let certain images pass before the mind. Lying on the ground relaxed and with the power of attention heightened, one is able easily to watch Christ's reactions in a variety of scenes. St. Ignatius was anxious that we would read the gospel passage first or have the history explained to us so that we keep closely to the facts. Next, he recommends the observation of the people first before listening to what they are saying or to the way in which they act. He does not seem to require any deep thought on our part, merely the spontaneous reactions of eyewitnesses.

As the right mental image of success will improve a tennis service, so a right image of virtue, by the lake side, at supper, with the sick or with the children, will eventually produce the required confidence. Unlike auto-suggestion which is often at fault, imaginative contemplation of the gospels provides an image of behavior that is Christian and capable of bewildering results. My mind turns to Francis Xavier in Japan or to John de Brebeuf among the Canadian Indians, for it was this method of Christo-cybernetics that alone explains their motive and the heroism of their lives. I find in field work that it is virtually impossible after lying down on the floor and just watching Christ with little children to get up and behave otherwise.

Once, years ago, I read somewhere a description of the prayer of St. Jane Frances de Chantal but this passage I have never since been able to trace. She herself was a prolific correspondent and a great many books have been written about her, so I have come to doubt the value of further search. According to this missing account, Jane Frances, when she was a widow caring for her little children, would read a gospel passage carefully. Next, she would picture the scene with elaborate care, noting

Christ, the disciples, the crowd, the centurion in the foreground, and would then listen to his act of faith. She would study his expression and the reactions of the crowd, ponder his words and their meaning in the imaginative setting that she had composed. Here was her backcloth. Weeks later, she had only to recall the scene and say, "Lord, I am not worthy," and the content of the centurion's prayer flooded back. Later she found that she had only to say the one word "Lord," and she could pray as he had; finally, she said no words but allowed the scene to calm her until she became the Centurion.

Jane Frances de Chantal became a woman of prayer and, years later, she made a curious observation which may perhaps be linked with this pictorial form of prayer: "I have come to see that I do not limit my mind enough simply to prayer, that I always want to do something myself in it, wherein I do very wrong. . . . I wish most definitely to cut off and separate my mind from all that, and to hold it with all my strength, as much as I can, to the sole regard and simple unity. By allowing the fear of being ineffectual to enter into the state of prayer and by wishing to accomplish something myself, I spoil it all."

9.

Face to Face

PART of the charm of field work lies in its incompleteness; one discovery opens the path to another and the search continues without end. Our bird watchers have been coming to the Isles of Scilly for decades without apparently exhausting the subject or themselves. Deep-sea divers never tire, for their hopes never fade. No sooner have the archeologists uncovered one burial chamber than they are out prospecting for the next. Most field workers take notes. Where the observations from previous trips have been written up and sifted, current jottings, hard to decipher, are studded with question marks.

Field work in prayer observes the same pattern with mystery following mystery and the solution to one problem triggering off the next. This final chapter must, then, be hesitant and inconclusive, for I have now reached the scribbled jottings which will lead the way to more research. Clear-cut solutions, neat conclusions, slick definitions would be dishonest, for prayer is an unending subject buried in eternity. Here we have no exact science which may be computerized or tabulated but a subtle form of art. We may best compare prayer to music, a kindred subject, full of rich surprises and as self-replenishing as the widow's cruse.

Field work in any sphere is based on personal observation and its conclusions are personal. One reaches decisions for one's own satisfaction and these may not be imposed on anyone else. Such decisions and conclusions have been set out in the early chapters of this book. It may help to epitomize them here before passing on into unknown territory. The first and most important is that there can be no substitute for private, secret prayer. The reason for this has been stated by David Wilkerson in his *The Cross and the Switchblade,* an account of his work with voluntary helpers in the New York slums. "Each morning these young men and women would rise, have breakfast and then spend the morning in prayer and study; it would be an essential part of our work. I had long discovered that too much running around without a base of quiet meditation produces little of value."

My second conclusion, based on Christ's injunctions, is that secret prayer must be conducted without a babble of words. Fulfillment, purposefulness, spiritual satisfaction is somehow attained by this silent confrontation with God. Thirdly, I now know that such private prayer will rarely prove successful without preparation and that such preparation may demand radical alteration in our way of life. Thus manual work, household chores, the right use of leisure may play a significant role in private prayer. Nor will we pray well for long without purposeful reading from as wide a field as possible. Fourthly, I have come to see that reading and relaxation must lead us towards full attention, that discipline of mind which enables us to hold ourselves suspended before turning all our faculties towards the chosen point. I have noted that yoga and other forms of bodily relaxation assist in producing such discipline. Fifthly, I am forced to admit that the chief threat to secret prayer comes from mental fragmentation and that, in reading, conversation, radio and television, one must steer well clear of theme-less trivia. A final lesson is taught by the saints, the importance of liberty of spirit, the willingness in private prayer to shed all discretion and to be guided only by reverence. Time, posture, methods of prayer must suit the individual and should be chosen for this end alone.

What Is the End of Prayer?

So simple a question as this may sound silly and its answer obvious. Yet in the earlier chapters of this book, I have quoted a variety of solutions and descriptions which reveal its complexities. You may recall St. Paul's formula: "This first of all, I shall ask," he wrote to Timothy, "that petition, prayer, entreaty and thanksgiving should be offered for all men." Another Paul, Blessed Paul Giustiniani, gave a more personal answer; his end in prayer was: "I adore, I honor, I thank, I appeal, I await, I desire." Ignatius of Loyola tells us to stand "with mind raised high and consider how God sees me and I will make an act of reverence and humiliation." Thomas More's secret prayer was made up of sorrow and thanksgiving like one "giving up his reckoning unto God of his sinful living." Or there was Radhakrishnan's less personal approach: "There are those who wish to see God face to face, others who delight in the endeavor to know the truth of it all." In these and a great many other statements, we see many paths leading to the same destination, the Burning Bush.

That God is the end of prayer may sound trite and obvious but it is also a fact that is ignored. Not a few people pray to benefit themselves. I am not here referring to that sense of courage and contentment which those obtain who seek such a perfect end. No, there is a more positive type of selfishness. A man who practices prayer simply to shed his own worries is, surely, thinking chiefly of himself. One whose sole aim in prayer is relaxation uses yoga as a gymnastic exercise. The same criticism would apply to those who adopt other forms of relaxation such as the one taught to me by Drs. Richardson and Boome. I was aware of this danger at the time. Again, prayer based on psycho-cybernetics and other forms of auto-suggestion may have no more than personal success as their goal. Some who attempt the emptying-out of self to induce Nirvana may attain a consider-able contentment without finding God. I myself sensed this self-centeredness in much of the Quietist literature. That many Quietists were undoubtedly ardent and sincere hardly justifies a method which makes us too preoccupied with our personal holi-ness. The end of prayer must be God himself and God alone. Our acts of sorrow, faith and love are really acts of worship and worship is the cornerstone. Augustine remarks that the act of adoration of a sinner is an act of contrition; one might say as well that a prayer of thanksgiving is the act of adoration of a grateful man.

The supreme example of selfishness in prayer, of using prayer for unworthy motives, is the act of petition which aims at ma-terial advantage for ourselves. For a large number of people, this asking for favors is the only form of prayer that they know. Yet prayer of petition is not wrong and Christ on many occa-sions both used and encouraged it. The Lord's prayer itself is filled with requests. The right and wrong use of prayers of peti-tion deserves consideration, for here we may study the right and wrong attitude in prayer. When we speak of prayer, we speak of four activities which must be blended to express our mood. In many old-time books on prayer these activities were labelled petition, intercession, adoration, and contemplation; and we may use the same titles now. The ascent to God is achieved by these four operations which cannot be kept in water-tight compart-ments and used by themselves. Some are inclined to speak in this way as though petition was for freshmen and contempla-tion reserved for higher grades. Such rigidity is wrong. Many grave old saints with great experience in prayer fell back on prayers of petition while not a few young saints were contemplatives from the start. Prayer, like music, may change from moment to moment, now profound, now lighthearted, but with the theme the same. The deeper one's prayer, the more simple it becomes, the more integrated, until the barriers between vocal and mental, contemplative and mental fall away. Aldous Huxley in his *Perennial Philosophy* stresses this urgent point: "Psychologically, it is all but impossible for a human being to practice contemplation without preparing for it by some kind of adoration and without feeling the need to revert at more or less frequent intervals to intercession or some form of petition."

Petition

Asking favors for oneself, either spiritual or material, is in no way selfish if such petition is blended with the adoration of God. We ask, as C. S. Lewis was quoted as saying, not because we want to force God to heed us, but merely to tell him that this seems important to us. All friendship supposes such openness. The trouble with prayer of petition is that it can easily be divorced from intercession, adoration and contemplation to be used as an end in itself. The man who adores God may be moved to ask for some favor, but one who asks for favors may omit adoration through self-centeredness. As Huxley puts it, "Petitionary prayer may be used—and used, what is more, with what would ordinarily be regarded as success—without any but the most perfunctory and superficial reference to God in any of his aspects. To acquire the knack of getting his petitions answered, a man does not have to know God or love him or even to know or love the image of God in his own mind. All he requires is a burning sense of the importance of his own ego, coupled with the firm conviction that there exists out there in the Universe, something not himself which can be wheedled or dragooned into satisfying these desires. If I repeat 'My will be done' with the necessary degree of faith and persistency, the chances are that sooner or later and somehow or other I shall get what I want."

Intercession

Prayer of petition has its dangers when its end is not the glory of God. Prayer of intercession may also be poisoned by self-promotion but not so easily. We intercede for others and hence such requests as we make stem often from charity. The Bible is rich in examples of such intercession, from Abraham's effort to save Sodom to Moses with his hands raised during a battle to the endless sacrifices in the Temple, interceding for mankind. This note of intercession is central to the life of Christ.

The full significance of prayers of intercession is seen in that form of awareness which some Oriental writers call cosmic consciousness. By means of prayer a self-conscious man gradually sheds his self-centerdness. He becomes deeply committed to the world around him and increasingly identified with life in all its myriad forms. This we may see in the Psalms. Much of what David wrote now sounds mildly suburban, dealing, as it does, with local enemies and "small-town" wars. Yet running through the Psalms is a wider theme of intercession, linking men by the bonds of fellowship with each other and with the trees, rivers, mountains, sun, moon and stars. Greater than man by himself is mankind as a unity; and mankind taken by itself is not as impressive as mankind in its true evolutionary setting at the apex of the universe. St. Paul, in many startling passages of great beauty, seems to be pointing to this cosmic consciousness. Not only does he write feelingly of God's master plan and of Christ's unique position in all creation but he has a note of cosmic intercession in his thought. Does he not suggest that man is responsible not only for his own salvation but for his race, his world, his universe?

In an earlier chapter, while discussing books that might lead us "to Godwards," I proposed the widest field of reading as an aid to prayer. Behind this suggestion lay the majestic theme of universal intercession so well expressed by Père Teilhard de Chardin in our day. The more one studies astronomy or man's journey into space, the more one reads of primitive animal life and its slow development, the easier is the advance to Godwards and the escape from selfish prayer. Teilhard de Chardin was a man of prayer but his prayer was cosmic-conscious, with a vocabulary unknown to the mystics of any previous age. His life-time moved from the horrifying slaughter of the First World War trenches to the plains of China and his *Hymn of the Universe*. As with St. Paul, Teilhard de Chardin strikes a note of cosmic intercession, with Christ at the center of all creation and interceding for us still. Like Paul, he sees "the puzzling reflections in a mirror" and interprets them. Both Paul and Teilhard glimpse the further plan behind all creation, both introduce a note of cosmic intercession, both seem to have a secret clue to the mystery of the Unknown God.

Prayer of intercession if thus widened and extended adds a new dimension to prayer in one's private room. Teilhard prayed thus: "Now, Lord, through the consecration of the world, the luminosity and fragrance which suffuse the universe, take on for me the linaments of a body and face—in you. What my mind glimpsed through its hesitant explorations, what my heart craved with so little expectation of fulfillment, you now magnificently unfold for me: the fact that your creatures are not merely so linked together in solidarity that none can exist unless all the rest surround it but that all are so dependent on a single, central reality that a true life, born in common by them all, gives them ultimately their consistence and their unity. Shatter, my God, through the daring of your revelation the childishly timid outlook that can conceive of nothing greater or more vital in the world than the pitiable perfection of our human organism. On the road to a bolder comprehension of the universe, the children of this world day by day outdistance the masters of Israel; but do you, Lord Jesus, in whom all things subsist, show yourself to these who love you, as the Higher Soul and physical center of your creation."

Field work in prayer may lead many of us to a deeper study of Teilhard de Chardin who stands on the very threshold of a new approach to prayer. He was charged with pantheism in his day. What to me is more clear is that, in his bold search for Truth, he drew very near to the ancient, Oriental style of contemplation and there are striking similarities between his approach to God and that expressed in Hindu literature. My attention was called to the verses of Rabindranath Tagore, the great modern Indian poet, who so constantly returns to Teilhard's theme. "The vitality that flows in waves, night and day, through every vein of my body, flows out to conquer the universe; pulsates through the world in amazing rhythm and cadence; inspires every pore of the earth's soil with the thrill of a million grass-blades growing; blossoms into flowers and young leaves; sways, year after year, in the ceaseless ebb and flow of the undulating world-wide sea of life and death.

"That endless vitality, absorbed into my being, exalts me in every limb. In my veins dances today that vast rhythm of aeons."

Contemplation

In the traditional ascent to God, adoration is listed before contemplation, which was always regarded as at the apex of all prayer in the heart. For purely personal reasons I reverse the order; my field work persuades me so to do.

In approaching the subject of contemplation, it may prove easiest to advance by slow stages, avoiding too much theory, for field work is not directly concerned with this. We may find all the theories in the books. What we seek now is practice and this must be based on personal experience. A notional assent to God is not sufficient to bring prayer to life. We have to behave as though God really existed and is present in the room. Christ said as much and we have already seen how the saints began all prayer with the injunction, "Put yourself in the presence of God." The point is important and to drive home its lesson, let me draw an illustration from an unusual source. When Douglas Hyde, the communist, decided to become a Catholic, he and his wife had for years lived without God. Now, they read up all the books and assimilated all the theories without finding the conviction that they sought. "Then one night as we ate our supper, I said that I thought that we should face up to reality, either we should abandon the whole business or we should be prepared to take an act of faith. Even as I said it I remembered the derisive definition of faith that I had so often quoted in the past; faith is that thing which enables us to believe that which we know to be totally untrue. As had so often been the case in recent years, I felt as though I was cut in two, two Douglas Hydes or two consciences urging conflicting lines of thought and action. One half of me supported my suggestion as being the obvious one, the other derided it, drew back instinctively as from something degrading. I heard my

126

voice saying, 'It is five to ten and we still don't believe in God as a living reality. In five minutes time, at ten o'clock, let's start. Let's act and think as though there really was one.' "

After reaching this decision, it took Douglas Hyde a month or two to find the reality that he sought. In almost every life, some such decision must be faced. Even for those who pray faithfully and whose acknowledgement of God is enduring, some small but definite decision must be reached at the start of prayer. A real assent to God is required for real prayer.

Some may ask, "Why need I bother with contemplation? Why can't I pray in secret in the old familiar way? My answer must be that we are under no obligation to change our methods and should pray in the style that comes to us most naturally. If vocal prayer or the use of psalms or of imaginative pictures of the gospel story help us better, we should cling to them. In prayer there should be no change for change's sake. Still more damaging would be change introduced for snobbish reasons, based on the erroneous premise that contemplation is a certain sign of holiness. We change or abandon methods simply because they no longer suit us; we have grown out of them. We find ourselves growing listless and inattentive and our thoughts and imaginative pictures tire us excessively. In his *Ascent to Mount Carmel,* St. John of the Cross provides a list of such symptoms as seem to suggest a change in prayer.

In prayer few changes are violent. We need reach no vigorous decisions but discover little by little that we pray better sitting than kneeling, best when prostrate on the ground. Again, though we cannot abandon thought in prayer, we find that it pays to transfer our thought to spiritual reading or to those quiet minutes when we perform our household chores. In this way, the time of prayer is more free and less cluttered; we are able to move more slowly and to sit quietly with God. In ordinary, everyday life, at home or with friends, we enjoy a similar pleasure when all the dusting, folding, letter-writing is completed and we may sink into the sofa with a sigh. "Thank God, I am free at last," we say with deep satisfaction, knowing that now we may give full attention to the person whom we love.

The Prayer of Simple Regard, as it is called, enshrines this sense of loving rest. Whether the physical relaxation calms the mind or a peaceful mind relaxes the body I cannot say. The two happen together anyway. Undoubtedly, a spell of relaxation, as has been explained, greatly aids in the control of breathing and this in turn induces that restful state of full attention and partial sleep. For those who love God and desire to love him more, such a state will foster a sense of security and friendship and an awareness which grows more and more acute. In itself this state of repose is not necessarily spiritual and may be enjoyed in some measure by those who admit no religious beliefs. For this reason *The Prayer of Simple Regard* is accepted by most authorities as natural. Whatever the degree of Divine grace —and few who have experienced this style of prayer would doubt God's assistance—*The Prayer of Simple Regard* may be induced. We remain in control of ourselves and may start or stop our prayer as we wish. Here is the only form of contemplative prayer available through our natural powers and dependent on ourselves. There is no danger of overdoing this form of prayer and many have used it constantly for years.

In such a restful form of prayer, words tend to get fewer and more simple following the normal moods of human love. As Clifton Wolters puts it, "A man and woman in love with each other have a lot to say in the early stages of their courtship but, as their love deepens, so the inadequacy of their thought and language about each other becomes more apparent and they have to speak in shorter, more pregnant and meaningful phrases but much less flowery than the earlier expressions. More would be neither sincere nor true. Something analogous characterizes the developing, simplifying prayer. The soul is now in love with God and more tongue-tied. This stage of prayer is called *affective,* not because the affections are aroused in an emotional way (that can happen but it is comparatively rare) but because the expression of prayer is basically affective or loving, even when the soul feels dry or desolate."

Those drawn to this *Prayer of Simple Regard* will find it fully described by St. Teresa of Avila in a hundred different places, by St. Jane Frances de Chantal who is regarded as its chief exponent, and by Père Poulain in the opening chapters of his great book. For myself, I do not find it helpful to read about secondhand experiences. Far better is it to lie or sit back quietly and to note the ease with which one may rest before God. Thoughts grow fewer, words slower and far more significant. So pleasing and restful is this style of prayer that those who enjoy it begin to wonder whether or not they are deceiving themselves. Reared in the business and activity of vocal, mental or liturgical prayer, they fear that this peaceful type of prayer is sheer laziness. When such misgivings arise, then is the time to study the description of *The Prayer of Quiet* bequeathed to us by so many saints. Too much study of mystic prayer without any experience tends to make us too self-conscious and complacent, even hypocritical. Christ said that God would reward us if we pray in secret and we should not attempt by imagination to hurry him. Those who read about mystic states often are led to self-persuasion and this is dangerous.

The Prayer of Simple Regard is generally not regarded as mystical in the fullest sense. For this reason one may best concentrate on this style of prayer to which by love and desire we may all attain. Mystical prayer by definition supposes a direct intervention by God who may limit or restrict our natural pow-ers and lead the soul by strange, supernatural ways. As with *The Prayer of Simple Regard,* it seems to me far safer to ex-perience such intervention first than to read about it, for there are few fields in which it is more easy by auto-suggestion to delude ourselves.

Mystical Prayer

Certain very obvious problems confront us when we consider mystical prayer. In the first place, the experiences enjoyed differ with the individual recipients, as may be seen in the accounts left by so many saints. Next, for one who prays alone, the con-tact with God is achieved with no witness present to report the event. The suspicion is always present to the mystic that he or she is fooling herself. St. Teresa in her fourth relation to her confessor put this puzzlement very well: "However confidently they assured her that God was at work within her, she never believed it so resolutely as to be able to swear to it, though from the effects produced and the great favors wrought in her, she judged that some of these things must have been caused by a good spirit." Teresa expresses her doubts frequently. Again, lan-guage is a problem after some unusual experience. Some efforts have been made to formalize a contemplative vocabulary but with small success. Père Poulain in his *The Graces of Interior Prayer* has analyzed mystical prayer in all its phases but at sec-ondhand. The saints who enjoyed these experiences lived long before Père Poulain and could not consult him before writing them down. We have seen how Ignatius of Loyola used the word "contemplation" in a new and imaginative sense. Miss Laski, in her study of ecstasy, includes accounts of natural and amorous absorption which would not be accepted in strictly religious books. *Nirvana,* "the passionless imperturbability," as one writer calls it, means something very different for a Buddhist than for a Christian with his more positive concept of God. Again, in describing the union with God, some of the mystics fall back on the language of human lovers, sometimes with strange and embarrassing results. Such expressions as "spiritual nuptials" sound bad enough but are reduced to the ridiculous when an artist, however famous, attempts to depict them with his brush.

In the hands of the secular writers, the very word "mystic" has been badly mauled. Thus my dictionary sees it as standing for poetic, obscure, spiritually significant or symbolic, occult, mysterious. When it comes near to the strict, religious meaning of the word, my dictionary adds an inaccurate detail: "A mystic. One who claims to attain or believes in the possibility of attaining insight into mysteries transcending ordinary human knowledge as by immediate intuition in a state of spiritual ecstasy."

Such confusion of thought and language, easily understandable, has made a mystic into one off-balance and presented contemplation as both snobbish and exceptional. In current parlance, a contemplative is a member of a religious congregation which leaves the world to lead a life of prayer enclosed. We meet, time and time again, the odd distinction between saints who were merely active and those chosen ones who were contemplative. Were I to ask, "Was Thomas More contemplative? Was Teilhard de Chardin a mystic?", many experts would have to hum and haw. As I have already said, we need frequently to remind ourselves of the simplicity and very ordinariness of so many of the greatest mystics and saints. I write this not to belittle them or to pretend that contemplative prayer is easy but merely to avoid that inferiority complex which might persuade us to set our sights too low. Contemplation is not

necessarily linked with ecstasy or with mysticism as my dictionary suggests, nor is ecstasy a sure sign of sanctity. Clifton Wolters in his admirable introduction to *The Cloud of Unknowing*
stresses this point: "Almost without exception," he writes, "the
masters of the spiritual life warn us against making ecstasy a
sign of spirituality and suggest that it should never be sought
for and discounted if it comes."

A further complication has to be faced after the sixteenth
century, the astonishing cult of the great Spanish mystics, St.
Teresa of Avila and St. John of the Cross. Their approach to
prayer has been so widely accepted that true contemplation has
today been restricted to those who assume their outlook and
conform to their rules. Far be it from me to seem to speak
slightingly of two such recognized masters of prayer. Yet how
great would be the error in seeking to identify contemplation
with the Spanish mystics or in trying to suggest that John of
the Cross or Teresa of Avila enjoyed some spiritual superiority.
With the glory of God and the worship of God as the end of
all contemplation, who would dare to adjudicate between prayer
and prayer? By identifying the highest forms of prayers with
contemplative orders or with the two great Spanish mystics, the
Western Church may have discouraged thousands with a different but equally effective form of prayer. St. Teresa was exceptional in her diffidence and as hesitant as anyone else.

One last important note may be added about mystical prayer.
A great many experts, J. V. Bainvel and Clifton Wolters among
them, emphasize the fact that prayer is often a matter of temperament. Bainvel, writing the introduction to the tenth edition
of Père Poulain's book, has this to say: "It seems impossible to
deny that certain temperaments seem more fitted for the unfolding of the mystical states. By this I do not mean only the
physical temperament but the moral, the turn of mind, the dis-

positions of the heart. Affective souls, delicate and refined, re-
flective and interior, of nervous temperament, almost morbid,
are not all mystics but they show some mystic tendencies."
Wolters goes rather further and admits that ecstasy and other
psycho-physical phenomena "depend more on temperament and
psychical make-up than on the visit of God itself." If this is
true, as I believe it to be, and if a certain style of prayer suits
only a certain type of temperament, then we must suppose a
more general and ordinary form of contemplation, equally fruit-
ful, equally "to Godward" for those who are not refined, nervous, affective, morbid but who love God with all their hearts.
Ultimately, it is love that brings us to God and love is a very
personal commodity.

The Ascent by Analogy

In the I.Q. tests used in most schools, the perception of each
candidate is scrutinized by questions based on analogy. You and
I are familiar with the type of question which asks, "*Candy* is
to *boy* what ——— was to Eve?" Like this one, so many queries in the tests seemed silly and yet the ability to spot similarities and to jump from the known to the unknown was often
decisive for true progress at school. In the years when I taught
boys, I found that a facility with analogies, metaphors and similes marked off the thoughtful boy. A similar gift distinguishes
the poet and author and is essential for a good teacher or orator.
The point is only made here because of its bearing on contemplative prayer.

When I sit back relaxed with God or yearning to find him,
my heart and mind may make an ascent through analogies. In
ordinary mental prayer it is the mind that finds the compari-
sons, but in contemplation the heart senses this bond. Take the
mind first. It becomes clear over the years, through reading and

experience, that God lies well beyond the capacity of human thought. The older mystical approach, called the *Via Positiva,* gladly admitted this incapacity. God might be described positively by the use of human analogies, but these had to be infinitely enlarged. "Though inexpressibly beyond all human understanding of these terms," writes Clifton Wolters, "there is still a connection between the human significance and the divine and the difference is quantitative rather than qualitative. Broadly speaking, this is the biblical view and though it lays itself open to the charge of making God in man's image, its safeguard is in the teaching that man is made to God's image and that our virtues and graces are but a reflection of his."

So much for thought and the acknowledgment of analogies which link our lives with God's. The heart need not think out such matters but surrenders to them sensibly. It senses love. One of the easiest of such analogies, much favored by certain mystics and drawn from the Song of Solomon, extends to God the relationship on earth between a boy and a girl. The boy-girl similes are attractive, simple, easy to follow while love itself is, in a sense, irrational, intuitive, beyond the realm of thought. In a way we are out of our minds when we love. All the acts of human love from wooing to surrender, from surrender to fusion, from fusion to satisfaction, are sufficiently beyond the scope of reason to be described as ecstasy. Miss Laski takes cases from human love and cases from religious writings when compiling her book. Human love is not directly a thought process but relies on sensation, emotion, touch. Mystics of certain schools and in certain epochs seem to overdo this preoccupation with love. True, they raise such love to an infinite degree and warn us of the dangers of imagination without quite freeing prayer from emotional excess. Writing of such love, Teilhard de Chardin remarks, "I know from experience how for the most part these words evoke in non-Christians either a kindly or malicious incredulity. The idea of loving God and the world, they object, is surely a psychological absurdity. How is one in fact to love the intangible, the Universal?"

While lying tranquil in *The Prayer of Simple Regard,* it will pay us handsomely to vary and deepen our analogies. There are other relationships beyond the reach of thought, experienced intuitively, and perhaps more enduring than those of the lover and the beloved. Each for himself in this. It is the sensing of this bond, not thoughts about it, that may lift us from the ground. The security of a baby on his parent's lap is a simile much favored. "I allow myself with delight," writes Teilhard, "to be cradled in the Divine fantasy." In a letter from the Tower of London, More wrote, "God dangleth me on his lap like a little boy." I myself would always maintain that this intuitive sense of love and security, known by infants in the natural order, is a more enduring and apt analogy than the Canticle of Canticles when applied to God. For this reason, the word "father," not thought about but felt, may be found as the true foundation for most Christian prayer. Even this analogy, basic as it is, cannot tell the whole tale. From Christ's extraordinary analogy in the story of the Prodigal Son, we may work backwards and downwards through the Bible narrative to the shepherd with his sheep, so dear to David, and to Jeremiah's great comparison between the potter and his clay. "We are," writes C. S. Lewis in *The Problem of Pain,* "not metaphorically, but in very truth, a Divine work of art, something that God is making and therefore something with which he will not be satisfied until it has a certain character." As I get older I grow more attached to mobile analogies through which the present energy, interest and action of God is more aptly displayed. God is fashioning us now, feeding and protecting us in the present moment, in a true sense creating and rearing us today. So many of the analogies in the psalms are alive, thousands of years after they were first written and put to music; the doe is still running to the fountain and the cedar is refreshed. Augustine has an analogy of harmony in music ringing in the ear. Teilhard de Chardin finds his analogies in science and his harmonies in the universe: "At this moment when your life has just poured with superabundent vigor into the Sacrament of the world, I will savor with heightened consciousness the intense yet tranquil rapture of a vision whose coherence and harmonies I can never exhaust."

The use of analogy in our search for God, however inadequate, is valid and fully justified. Why, even in this life, men cannot meet or become aware of one another without a common tel-star off which to bounce their thoughts. "People often talk," writes C. S. Lewis, "as if nothing were easier than for two naked minds to 'meet' and become aware of each other. But I see no possibility of their doing so except in a common medium which forms their 'external world' or environment. Even our vague attempts to imagine such a meeting between disembodied spirits usually slips in, surreptitiously, the idea of, at least, a common space and a common time, to give the *co* in *co-existence* a meaning; and space and time are already an environment. But more than this is required. If your thoughts and passions were directly presented to me, like my own, without any mark of externality or otherness, how should I distinguish them from mine? And what thoughts or passions could we begin to have without objects to think and feel about? Nay, could I even begin to have the conception of 'external' and 'other' unless I had experience of an 'external world'?" This quotation pleases me greatly and provides much thought. In reaching out to God through analogy or metaphor, we are not surrendering to wishful thinking or romancing in any way. We are using our minds and hearts in an honest manner, in the way that we have to use them when communicating among ourselves. There is no other way. Again, it is worthwhile noting how Lewis talks about thoughts and passions, using passion in the context with no sinful or compulsive connotation but as an expression of those mutual feelings which we all experience away from thought. In meditation, we may think about the bonds of Fatherhood, Love, Harmony, Truth which lead us to Godwards, but in contemplation we feel and experience them.

Let me end my section on analogy in prayer with a quotation from St. Augustine who, in my opinion, comes nearer than any other to expressing its depth. As so often in his *Confessions* the great doctor is addressing God himself. He puts the question which each of us in our field work may answer for ourselves.

"What is it that I love when I love thee? Not the beauty of any bodily thing nor the order of the seasons nor the brightness of light that rejoices the eye nor the sweet melodies of all songs nor the fragrance of flowers and ointments and spices; nor manna nor honey, not limbs that carnal love embraces. None of these things do I love in loving my God.

"Yet, in a sense, I do love light and melody and fragrance and food and embrace when I love my God; the light and the voice and the food and the fragrance and the embrace in the soul when that light shines upon my soul which no place can contain, that voice sounds which no time can take away, I breathe a fragrance which no wind scatters, I eat a food which is not lessened by the eating and I lie in an embrace which satiety never comes to sunder. This is it that I love when I love my God."

Dennis the Areopagite

We started our field work with St. Paul at Athens, in a city drawn to novelties and superstitious enough to add to its many

137

idols an altar to the Unknown God. Invited to the Council of the Areopagus, the Apostle of the Gentiles drew his inspiration from this altar and addressed the councillors about their Unknown God. His preamble ended: "Well, the God whom I proclaim is, in fact, the one whom you already worship without knowing it."

Paul's sermon was a partial success. When he spoke boldly about the Resurrection, "some of them burst out laughing; others said, 'We would like to hear you talk about this again.'" Paul left the assembly with their sophisticated laughter ringing in his ears. His address was not, however, a total failure, for a few in his audience and in Athens followed him. We read: "There were some who attached themselves to him and became believers, among them Dionysius, the Areopagite."

A short diversion may not be out of place. This Dionysius, later famous as Dennis the Areopagite, became a name to conjure with in Western prayer. Centuries after those who had mocked St. Paul had been forgotten, he enjoyed international fame. By a curious quirk of history, his reputation was founded on a book that he almost certainly did not write. His *Mystical Theology* is thought to have been composed in the sixth century by an unknown Syrian monk. It was not uncommon in ancient times for an author to take as *nom de plume* some distinguished forebear and our unknown monk may have believed that he was passing on Dionysian thought. His little book was a summary of Eastern mysticism with the added, semi-apostolic authority of Dennis's name. Over the centuries, *Mystical Theology* was translated into Latin and, though it started slowly, eventually became in every part of Europe the best and most respected manual on contemplative prayer. Even today the theory, if not the book, is widely accepted and serves as an ecumenical link with the Greek Church.

The views of prayer attributed to Dennis may best be studied in more learned books than this. Our chief interest here and the point which affected my field work is the seeming contradiction between the *Via Negativa* of Dennis and the *Via Positiva* of analogous prayer. Where the traditional view had brought us to God by raising our human attributes to infinite proportions, the Oriental approach began with the unknowability of God. Clifton Wolters outlines the theory thus: "God is 'wholly other' and qualitatively different from his creatures; they depend on him but not he on them. Creation contributes nothing to his fullness or his happiness; he is complete in himself and fundamentally beyond the power of any created intellect to comprehend. Any description, however exalted, is inevitably a human one, and because of this difference in kind can never be accurate or adequate. If we say that he is 'great' or 'most high' or is 'a person' or is 'good', we use words which can only be properly understood in a human context, words which distinguish 'you' from 'me' and each of us from the next man. Manifestly we cannot speak of Deity like that, for finite and temporal cannot stand over against the Infinite and Eternal. God cannot be great or high or personal or good in our sense of the words. He of whom the Positive Way would make many and glorious affirmations is so much more than these that we speak more truly when we say that he is none of them and is more worthily described negatively than positively. He cannot be understood by man's intellect. The truths of religion about him can, but not himself. When the mind faces him who is absolutely different, it 'seizes up'; it becomes blank before a knowledge it can never assimilate because it can never understand the first thing about it; it enters a cloud of unknowing."

The mention of this cloud of unknowing, the suggestion that a negative approach to God might be more true than a positive, may at first sound shocking to a pious soul. From the day when the voice of Dennis the Areopagite was heard, a strange, hard, ruthless note of servility and despair is introduced. Maybe, as I have found in my field work, such an attitude is salutary in the approach to God. The influence of the negative way is seen historically, spreading from author to author and country to country as Dennis was more widely recognized and approved. *The Cloud of Unknowing* is based almost entirely on his theory and to him we may attribute much of St. John of the Cross's vocabulary, purgation, the dark night of the senses, the dark night of the soul. Dom John Chapman, a modern authority on prayer, sounds the same note. He writes in a letter, "But in prayer always and out of prayer also—the mainspring of everything is wholly irrational, meaningless, inexpressible. I want God and the word 'God' has absolutely no meaning. I find so many in this positively absurd and obviously mystical condition; I suppose one contemplates without knowing it . . . the whole object of life becomes to want nothing that is not God. Only there is no reason for it. The word 'God' means nothing that we can think or conceive. . . . I have been instructing a good young monk how never to think about anything when he is praying."

Statements such as these, and they may be found in the writings of a great many mystics, Western and Oriental, may for a moment shatter our belief in prayer. Yet, when they are fully understood, they appear not only beautiful but as adding a new dimension to prayer. The *Via Negativa* is negative only in name. Dennis is really saying that the truths about God are so overwhelmingly positive and real that we cannot comprehend them or describe them with our human minds and limited vocabulary. "At no time," writes Clifton Wolters, "will he say that God is unknowable save to the power of the intellect and then only because it is limited. God can be known by love and by love the soul enters into union with him. The way that love is expressed and experienced is in prayer. Prayer is communion with God, leading to union."

In the early chapters of this book, I noted the difference between theory and practice, envying the good fortune of those naval cadets who spend three months in the classroom and then put to sea to test out the theories for themselves. So it is with prayer for the man who grasps that the confrontation with God in secret only becomes a theory when committed to paper and written up into a book. It first saw life as an experience. Neither the *Via Positiva* nor the *Via Negativa* have much value in theory; we must first do our field work and observe and experience them ourselves. When we have learned to relax, to read the right books, to avoid fragmentation, to practice both awareness and attention, then, when we pray to God in secret, our words will grow fewer, our thoughts less distracting, our aspirations more intense. The positive and negative approaches will blend together to form a prayer natural to ourselves. It seems probable to me from the example of many saints that part of our prayer will be by analogy, part thought, part sensation; for seconds and minutes at a time, totally unexpected, all thought will be driven out by love.

My field work over the years has led me to the study of the human machinery to locate the rendezvous with God. More and more during my life-time, the great psychologists have come to recognize the three dimensions of our lives. The mystics, in less professional language, knew of these for centuries. I need not attempt to cover so intricate a subject now. It will be sufficient only to point to our physical dimension, that sphere in which we reach out to what many would call the 'real' world. In language, this is the dimension covered by the active voice. On this plane we are active and creative, sometimes actors, always salesmen, putting ourselves across. It was in this concrete, visible plane that Christ walked after the Incarnation; on the same plane we honor and worship God liturgically. Any mystical experience on this plane—seeing visions, hearing voices, swooning in ecstasy—should be treated with the caution it deserves.

The same You and Me become different on our second dimension, the one covered in language by the passive voice and reflexive verbs. On this level we are less creative, more receptive, drinking in sensations, absorbing the beauty of the world about us and surrendering to the message of the arts. On this plane God may speak to us through books and meditation, by means of imaginative contemplation, already described. Intense experience in prayer may affect us on this level, if we enjoy an unusual temperament.

Deeper than our creative and reflexive levels, we begin to grasp a further sphere of living, covered in language by the word "heart." We speak of a heart-to-heart conversation, describe others as hard-hearted, broken-hearted, kind-hearted or say of ourselves, "I haven't the heart to tell him such and such." Recent heart transplants in surgery have removed all significance from the organ in our body which for so long was regarded by the ancients as the throne of all emotion and love. The word "heart," as used in literature, retains its meaning, but has lost its dwelling-place. One may describe it as psychological and I have been very much helped by William James's expression, "the red-hot point of consciousness." Such a phrase makes the heart alive and ardent in the present moment; as Christ said of it, "It is from the overflow of the heart that the mouth speaks."

I would like to end this section with a paragraph which I

penned some years ago in an earlier book: "To complete our search for self-knowledge, we must edge just one step further into the center of our inner world. Deep in the center of our heart, in a silent world beyond the reach of the senses and the imagination, the Capital I keeps probing, seeking for self-fulfillment and security. It is alone and working in the dark. For in the center of our being is a cloud of unknowing in which even thought itself seems to fade. Dr. Sherwood Taylor put it to us in this way. 'Perhaps deeper and less clearly apprehended are certain knowings which are not facts or desires, the knowing and turning to something changeless that is not seen or heard by sense or imagination; something that remains when the tumult of the mind is hushed, when even the I is still and waiting. In this region there are no words, no images but there is that to which every thought and fantasy and imagining and desire are subject.' "

Now, eight years later, I would not want to re-write my paragraph. In the red-hot point of consciousness the obscurity remains, the cloud of unknowing has not been lifted, but the Capital I waits far more patiently. It sees more clearly the blurred impression in the mirror and knows whom it is waiting for.

To my paragraph I would add one phrase, used centuries ago by an ancient mystic who spoke of himself as "adhering to the Divine Ground." On my islands, the imagery might be less poetic and we might think of a barnacle clinging to a boat. Of the act of Adoration no more need be said than this. Whether we sit or stand or kneel to express our adherence, our spirit is not resentful of the darkness as it lies flat out on the Divine Ground. I used to picture a God who descended visibly from heaven but now the analogy has changed. For we, in scriptural terms, are "like cedars beside the water," and cedars are nourished silently and secretly through their deeply buried roots.

* * *

As I watch the bird-watchers, divers, botanists arriving on the Isles of Scilly, I can but puzzle at those chance encounters which give us a life-time of interest. A stamp album on a birthday, a word of encouragement at school, a discarded novel in a cupboard may trigger off a life-long commitment and pursuit. One of the largest bookshops in the world began with a disappointment when a young man failed in the Indian Civil Service exam. He put up his unwanted books for sale and his advertisement brought in so many applications that he could one day move from his mother's kitchen in Hackney to impressive premises in Tottenham Court Road.

Almost by accident, thanks to a passing illness, I first made contact with the Unknown God. At the age of twenty, I caught a germ, akin to measles, which kept me in bed for about six weeks. To fill up the days, I read Miss Strickland's tomes on the Queens of England and studied the story of Henry VIII's six unhappy wives. A borrowed musical box provided background music, a highland lament and "There Is No Place Like Home." It chanced that the doctor, a Presbyterian, had a passion for all things Tudor and, from his collection, would bring each day a Holbein sketch to hang on my wall. So, with my musical box churning out its tunes and Miss Strickland providing endless gossip, I gazed at the portrait of Henry VIII and his luckless ladies and came at last to the Holbein sketch of Sir Thomas More. Thus began a life-long friendship with a fellow countryman and fellow townsman who had been executed on Tower Hill four hundred years before.

Now the story of More's death I had known for years but the secret of his life remained hidden for centuries, for one does not

144

look for a peculiar type of sanctity in a twice-married man, holding the highest offices of the State and, as a successful attorney,
earning as much as 50,000 dollars a year. Only in my life-time
have his love poems become known, poems which a boy might
have penned for his darling, poems which young Master More
directed to God. Now, too, we know More's prayer "in the secret
chamber of the mind, in the privy closet of the soul"; a prayer
which "with very affection speaketh unto God and in the most
lightsome darkness of contemplation, not only presenteth the
mind to the Father but also uniteth it with Him by unspeakable
ways which only they know who have essayed."

It was unusual enough to me to meet a successful, urbane man,
so much loved, so openly religious; the greater shock came with
the realization that for fifty years More was in love with God.
So, for the love of God, he parted from his darling children and
was ready to die in proof of it. As he wrote in the Tower of
London, a boy would die for his girl and by so doing part from
her for ever where he had only to die to have God for good.
More found the Unknown God. Though frightened of death, he
wanted to die, "for the essential substance of all celestial joy
standeth in the blessed beholding of the Glorious Godhead face
to face and this, no man may presume to look for or obtain in
this life."

Bibliography

Allison Peers, E., *Behind That Wall*, London, 1947.

Augustine, St., *Confessions*, translated by F. J. Sheed, London and New York, 1942.

Aurelius, Marcus, *Meditations*, Penguin Classics, 1964.

Basset, Bernard, *The Noonday Devil*, New York, 1968.

———, *Born for Friendship*, New York and London, 1965.

Caussade, J. P. de, *Abandoment to Divine Providence*, St. Louis, 1921.

Chapman, Dom John, *Spiritual Letters*, London and New York, 1959.

Dechanet, Dom J. M., *Christian Yoga*, London and New York, 1960.

Douglas, Dr. Mary, *Natural Symbols*, Cresset Press, 1970.

Graham, Dom Aelred, *Zen Catholicism*, London and New York, 1963.

Huxley, Aldous, *The Perennial Philosophy*, London and New York, 1969.

Hyde, Douglas, *I Believed*, New York and London, 1950.

James, William, *The Varieties of Religious Experience*, New York, 1958.

Knox, Ronald, *The Imitation of Christ* (translator), London and New York, 1959.

Laski, Marghanita, *Ecstasy*, Cresset Press, 1961.

Leclercq, Dom Jacques, O.S.B., *Alone With God*, London, 1962.

Lewis, C. S., *Letters to Malcolm*, London and New York, 1966.

———, *The Screwtape Letters*, London and New York, 1955.

———, *The Problem of Pain*, London and New York, 1943.

Loyola, St. Ignatius of, *Spiritual Excercises*, London, 1893; New York, 1954.

Maharishi Mahesh Yogi, *On the Bhagavad Gita*, Penguin Books, 1969.

Maltz, Maxwell, *Psycho-Cybernetics*, London, 1959.

More, St. Thomas, *Dialogue of Comfort*, New York and London, 1951.

Moretti, G., *The Saints Through Their Handwriting*, London, 1964.

Poulain, Père A., S.J., *The Graces of Interior Prayer*, London and St. Louis, 1950.

Radhakrishnan, *The Hindu View of Life*, London, 1927.

Rolle, Richard, *Selected Writings,* London, 1963.

Speer, Alfred, *Inside the Third Reich,* New York and London, 1971.

Spencer, Sidney, *Mysticism in World Religion,* London, 1963.

Tagore, Rabindranath, *One Hundred and One,* Asia Publishing House, 1966.

Taylor, F. Sherwood, *Two Ways of Life,* London, 1947.

Teilhard de Chardin, Pierre, S.J., *The Divine Milieu,* London and New York, 1964.

——, *Hymn of the Universe,* London and New York, 1965.

Teresa of Avila, St., *Complete Works,* London and New York, 1946.

Weil, Simone, *Waiting on God,* London and New York, 1959.

Wilkerson, David, *The Cross and the Switchblade,* Philadelphia, 1970.

Wolters, Clifton, *The Cloud of Unknowing* (Introduction), London, 1961.

Index

Abraham, 123

À Kempis, Thomas, 68–69 (on reading Scripture); 72

Allison Peers, E., 73–74, 85–86 (on the interior life); 98

Aloysius Gonzaga, St., 98

Alphonsus Rodriguiz, St., 101

Ambrose, St., 91

Anselm, St., 69

Augustine of Hippo, St., 26, 44, 48 (on desires in prayer); 66, 71–72 (on conversion); 83, 87 (on posture in prayer); 90 (on vision at Ostia); 94, 121, 136–137 (on prayer of analogy)

Aurelius, Marcus, 24

Bainvel, J. V., 132 (on mystical temperaments)

Baker, Augustine, O.S.B., 95

Bellarmine, St. Robert, 98

Benedict, St., 36, 65

Benson, Robert Hugh, 71

Bernadette Subirous, St., 15, 53, 88

Bernard, St., 36, 69, 83

Bonaventure, St., 69

Bonhoeffer, Dietrich, 35

Boome, Dr. E. J., 106–109, 112–113, 116, 121

Brebeuf, St. John de, 88, 116

Bunyan, John, 94

Caesar, 110

Carlyle, Thomas, 77

Caussade, J. P. de, S.J., 40, 44, 49, 70, 95

Chantal, St. Jane Frances de, 116–117 (on her prayer); 129

Chapman, Dom John, O.S.B., 71, 92, 95, 129, 140

Chesterton, G. K., 71

Cicero, 24, 71

Cloud of Unknowing, The (Anon.), 48, 65–66 (on few words in prayer); 72, 84 (on no discretion needed in contemplation); 101, 132, 140

Confucius, 18

Coué, Dr., 114 (on auto-suggestion)

Cromwell, 110

Curé of Ars (St. John Vianney), 34, 87

Dante, 111

David, King, 123, 135

Dechanet, Dom J. M., O.S.B., 35–36, 54, 57–60, 63, 88–90, 101 (on Christian yoga)

Dennis the Areopagite, 27, 138–140 (on mysticism)

Douglas, Mary, 19 (on Bantu and Pygmy liturgies)

Fox, George, 94

Francis of Assisi, St., 91–92, 111 (his influence on Western prayer); 101

Francis Xavier, St., 116

Frankl, Victor, 35

Gertrude, St., 92

Giustiniani, Blessed Paul, 57–58, 60–63 (on habits as a hermit); 90, 96, 120

Goodier, Alban, S.J., 100 (on method of prayer)

Graham, Dom Aelred, O.S.B., 24

Grou, Père, S.J., 70

Hammarskjöld, Dag, 35, 71

Henry VIII, 144

Hitler, Adolf, 114

Holbein, 144

Hopkins, Gerard Manley, S.J., 71

Horace, 72

Huxley, Aldous, 15 (*Devils of Loudon*); 35, 71. 122 (on petitionary prayer)

Hyde, Douglas, 126–127 (story of conversion)

Ignatius of Loyola, St., 22 (each different in prayer); 39 (the number of his letters); 44, 49 (on the Pater Noster); 54 (on disposing the soul); 54, 66–67, 69 (on reading the Gospel); 82 (on preparing for prayer); 87, 89–92 (on posture in prayer); 94, 98, 108–109 (on contemplation); 111, 120

James, William, 56, 58–59, 79, 93–94, 111, 142

Jeremiah the Prophet, 135 (his vision of potter)

Jerome, St., 71

John of the Cross, St., 58–59, 95, 115, 127, 132

John XXIII, Pope, 32

Joseph, St., 31

Knox, Ronald, 41, 71, 76 (translation of St. Paul)

Lafarge, Father, S.J., 71

Lawrence, Brother, 30, 53, 93 (unusual method of prayer); 97–98 (his influence in France); 100

Laski, Marghanita, 66, 134

Lenin, Nicolai, 13, 15

Lewis, C. S., 16, 22 (on Rose Macauley's methods); 129 (*Screwtape Letters*); 34, 47 (on prayer without words); 50–51 (on the Lord's Prayer); 71, 86 (on saints); 90 (on posture in prayer); 91, 97, 110–111, 122, 135–137 (on analogy in prayer)

Lucretius, 72

Luke, St., 68

Luther, Martin, 94

Macauley, Rose, 22 (on use of secondhand prayers)

Maharishi Mahesh Yogi, 38, 42, 57

Maltz, Maxwell, 113–114 (*Psycho-Cybernetics*)

Marie Hilda, S.N.D., 106

Margaret Mary, St., 94

Martindale, C. C., S.J., 71

Merton, Thomas, 34, 71

Milton, John, 111

Monica, St., 87

More, St. Thomas, 42 (on being busy); 43, 91 (on prayer in private room); 66, 87 (influence of Pico della Mirandola); 70 (on spiritual reading); 72, 78, 83, 89 (on length in prayer); 91 (the New Building); 100, 102 (on his form of prayer); 120, 131, 135 (from Tower of London); 144–145 (last thought)

Moses the Patriarch, 18, 73–74, 88, 123

Newman, John Henry Cardinal, 25, 71, 72, 76, 87

Osiris, 81

Pascal, 47

Paul the Apostle, St., 26–27 (in Athens); 31, 39–40, 44 (on seeing in a mirror darkly); 48, 68 (his vision); 74–78 (guide to reading); 82, 84–85 (on use of word "saint"); 105, 110, 120, 123–124, 138–139 (at Athens again)

Perrin, Père, 81

Peter the Apostle, St., 31, 42, 53

Peter of Alcantara, St., 97 (on tedium in prayer)

Pico della Mirandola, Giovanni, 66, 87, 89

Plato, 18, 81

Poulain, A., S.J., 71, 129–130, 132

Quoist, Michel, 22

Radhakrishnan, 26, 35, 83 (on prayer); 120

Richardson, Dr. M. A., 106–109, 112–113, 116, 121

Rolle, Richard (Hermit), 90

Sales, St. Francis de, 21, 47, 56, 70, 97, 108, 115

Savio, St. Dominic, 53, 98

Shakespeare, William, 78

Speers, Albert, 114

Spencer, Sidney, 18–19

Suso, Blessed Henry, 91

Stevenson, Robert Louis, 94

Strickland, Agnes, 144

Tagore, Rabindranath, 125

Taylor, F. Sherwood, 143

Teilhard de Chardin, Pierre, S.J., 19–20, 27, 31, 34, 71, 124–125, 131 (on cosmic intercession); 134–135

Temple, Archbishop of Canterbury, 43

Teresa of Avila, St., 14, 30, 39, 42–44, 47, 51, 54, 67, 84–85, 87, 90,

Teresa of Avila (*cont.*)
  94, 96–97, 100, 103, 129–130, 132
Thérèse de Lisieux, St., 94
Thomas Aquinas, St., 34, 54, 72
Timothy, St., 82, 120

Virgil, 24, 71

Waugh, Evelyn, 71
Weil, Simone, 19–21, 41 (on fear of confronting God); 50–51 (on the Our Father); 71, 79, 81 (on reading); 92, 98, 103
Wesley, John, 66
Wilkerson, David, 72, 119
Wolters, Clifton, 128, 132–134 (on contemplative prayer)

Zacheus, 53
Zebedee, 53